Praying Without Asking

Elizabeth Jewkes

ISBN-13: 978-1500360368
ISBN-10: 1500360368
Copyright © 2014 Elizabeth Jewkes
All rights reserved.

Published by:
Myrrh Tree Publishing
38, Bedford Avenue
Cheshire
CH65 6PJ

www.facebook.com/prayingwithoutasking

First published in Great Britain in 2014
Copyright © 2014

The moral right of the author has been asserted.
All rights reserved. Without limiting the rights under copyright reserved above, no part of this publication may be reproduced or transmitted in any form or by any means, electronic or mechanical including photocopying, recording or by any information storage and retrieval system, without the prior written permission of the copyright owner.

Cover design by Elizabeth Jewkes and Carina Ellerington

Contents

Introduction

1	Praying without asking	7
2	But doesn't the Bible tell us to ask?	17
3	Do we really need to ask?	28
4	So what if we prayed without asking?	41
5	How to pray	56
6	Not praying, but listening	70
7	How not to pray	83
8	The power of praise	87
9	Confession	101
10	Taking it further	117
11	Conclusion	128

Introduction

I became a Christian as a small child so prayer has been part of my life for as long as I can remember. In October 2011, a friend of mine asked me if I would prayer walk around the school where she worked. It seemed easy enough to change my early morning lying on the sofa quiet time for a walking round the neighbourhood one. I decided to take the dog with me and he was overjoyed to get a walk twice as far as he used to get. After about three months, God said to me "You know you say the same things everyday. Why don't you junk all of it and just praise?". Whaaat? Not ask for anything? Not tell God what I wanted him to do? Just praise? I soon realised that if I couldn't ask, then I would need to start trusting that God knows my situation, knows my concerns and can be relied on to do the best for me without being asked. And I'd need to change my prayer style from being predominantly about asking God to praying without asking
I gave it a try and it changed my life. This is my story.

Chapter 1 What's the point of prayer?

What does the Lord require of you? To act justly and to love mercy and to walk humbly with your God.
Micah 6 v 8

Ever sat in a prayer meeting listening to a long shopping list of wants? Ever felt uncomfortable when people just demand that God does this or that or tell him the solution they want? Ever squirmed as someone shouts, rants or shrieks their demands at God? Ever felt sad as a praying voice becomes increasing anxious or frazzled? Ever wondered if prayer has to be like this? Ever wondered if we actually have to tell God our problems? Ever thought that maybe an almighty God doesn't need telling what our problems are? Ever wished that we all asked less and thanked more? Ever wondered what it would be like to never need to ask for anything and instead to just trust God? For some time, I've become increasingly uncomfortable with the prayers I'm hearing. I hear too many shopping list prayers. I rarely hear God being thanked yet we keep asking so surely we think God will answer our prayers? But instead of thanking God for answered prayer we just move on to the next problem. This was highlighted for me recently when I attended a prayer meeting. The leader explained that the format of the meeting was simple, it would follow the acrostic ACTS, Adoration, Confession, Thanks, Supplication. We began with worship songs and went on to silent confession. The leader explained that we would begin our prayer time by thanking God for all the good things in our lives and asked a woman to begin. The prayer she prayed thanked God without asking for anything. So why did the group immediately plunge into asking prayers? Mine was the only other thankful prayer. It was almost as if thanking God was completely alien to those attending that prayer meeting. This isn't an unusual situation. I've seen it replicated so many times. Too many people only see prayer as a means to asking God for what we want or need. Prayer is so much more than that. Why do we pray? What does God want from us? Remember the film 'Bruce Almighty'? And if you haven't seen the film I wholeheartedly recommend it. God gives Bruce the power to do almost anything. He isn't allowed to do anything harmful, nor is he allowed to interfere with free will. So that mean he can't make people love him. Bruce, who knows he has screwed up his relationship with his girlfriend and wants her to love him, is disappointed by this. How can he get someone to love him? Bruce asks God. And God replies, "When you come up with the answer to that one, you let me know" is God's reply. Because this is the one thing that God doesn't do, he doesn't make people love him. He gives us a choice. So it's the one thing we can do for God. We can tell him we love him.

I did the Alpha course once for a group of mums from school. I asked them what they wanted most from their children. To be the cleverest

the most talented child in their class? Success is good, but surely what we want most of all is for our children to climb on our laps and tell us they love us. God is the same.
Micah puts it rather well. Micah 6 v 6-8 NIV

With what shall I come before the Lord and bow down before the exalted God? Shall I come before him with burnt offerings, with calves a year old? Will the Lord be pleased with thousands of rams, with ten thousand rivers of oil? Shall I offer my firstborn for my transgression, the fruit of my body for the sin of my soul?
He has shown you, O mortal, what is good. And what does the Lord require of you? To act justly and to love mercy and to walk humbly with your God.

Thousands of rams, ten thousand rivers of olive oil or the one and only firstborn. These are offerings on a grand scale. But are they what God wants? Micah doesn't think so. He doesn't want ten thousand rivers of olive oil or for us to sacrifice our firstborn children. He wants us to love him back. It's one thing we can give to God Micah suggests three more – acting justly, loving mercy and walking humbly with God. How does walking humbly with God fit in with the endless want lists our prayers often seem to be? It doesn't seem very humble to me to be telling God what we want, how we want it and when we want it. When prayers are nothing more than a huge 'I want' list, it's as if God is some spiritual Santa. I often wonder what God thinks when we only ask. When my kids ask for too much too often and fail to do anything for me, I tell them they're overdrawn on the bank of Mum. If they want me to do lots for them, they need to think about what I need help with and wash up or hoover, to act like they are part of the family, to take responsibility for caring for all of us. I think God feels the same. We shouldn't just ask, ask, ask. We should act like we are part of his family. If we only pray asking prayers, then the chances are we are endlessly repeating the same requests. Shouldn't we try trusting God and waiting for the answer? f our kids kept reminding us to do the stuff we do anyway how insulted would we feel? In Matthew 6 Jesus tells us to look at the flowers of the field and points out that is how God dresses grass. How much more does he care for us? Even the hairs on our head are numbered. This is fine detail attention. Do we really believe this? Or do we have doubts? I suspect that people who don't quite believe that God loves them struggle with this. I believe that there is nothing I can do to make God love me more and that there is nothing I can do to make God love me less. Do you believe this too?

Although I came to know God as a very small child, I am always aware of his status as the Almighty God, maker of heaven and earth. I get very upset in prayer meetings when I hear people shouting at God or demanding he does something, repeating what they want endlessly as if they're trying to batter him into submission. I

find it hard to reconcile Micah's call to 'walk humbly with your God' with endlessly asking God to do things and equally I certainly cannot reconcile it with shouting. I recently sat and squirmed in a church service while a man prayed for healing. He shouted at God to 'send fire' on the disease afflicting the person. Marching backwards and forwards across the church shouting SEND FIRE, SEND FIRE, SEND FIRE, SEND FIRE, SEND FIRE, SEND FIRE SEND FIRE, SEND FIRE, SEND FIRE, SEND FIRE. Are you bored yet? I was, but we aren't even halfway through yet.
SEND FIRE, SEND FIRE, SEND FIRE SEND FIRE, SEND FIRE, SEND FIRE.
I think we're about halfway now. He must have used that same phrase 30 times. Did he really think that sort of endless repetition improved the likelihood of God answering his prayer? Why would he think that? Perhaps he's read the parables Jesus told about the man who knocked on his neighbour's door or the widow and the unjust judge and took them to mean if you shout at God enough one evening, he'll do what you want. I think those stories are more about being persistent, believing that God will act, even when God seems to be ignoring us, rather than shouting a lot in one go. I can't see that God fits the description of an unjust judge or even that we are weak and powerless. To be honest, his prayer just made me cringe. In the Bible, it's the heathens who shout & repeat their prayers endlessly. Here's the story of when Elijah challenged the prophets of Baal. He told them

to prepare a sacrifice but not light it. If Baal was a real god, he should be able to send fire from heaven to light the sacrifice. The prophets of Baal agree, but it didn't go the way they hoped:

1 Kings 18:26-29 (Complete Jewish Bible)
They took the bull that was given to them, prepared it and called on the name of Ba'al from morning till noon — "Ba'al! Answer us!" But no voice was heard; and no one answered, as they jumped around on the altar they had made.
Around noon Eliyahu (Elijah) began ridiculing them: "Shout louder! After all, he's a god, isn't he? Maybe he's daydreaming, or he's on the potty, or he's away on a trip. Maybe he's asleep, and you have to wake him up."
So they shouted louder and slashed themselves with swords and knives, as their custom was, until blood gushed out all over them.
By now it was afternoon, and they went on ranting and raving until it was time for the evening offering. But no voice came, no one answered, no one paid any attention.

The 'send fire' ranting I sat through bore more than a passing resemblance to the story in 1Kings. Unfortunately it sounded more like the prophets of Baal. Elijah soaked his sacrifice and altar in water and even dug a trench to hold the water he poured on it all. But he only called on God once before fire fell and consumed the lot, sacrifice, water, even the stones. Let's not insult God with prayers like this.

When we pray are we telling God new information? Of course not. I don't have to tell God what's going on or even what I care about. He already knows it all.

So what is the point of prayer? Are we directing God to act in a way of our choosing? I hope not.

Isaiah 55:8-9 NIV
'For my thoughts are not your thoughts, neither are your ways my ways, 'declares the Lord. As the heavens are higher than the earth, so are my ways higher than your ways and my thoughts than your thoughts. Job ch 38 v 2-11 *And now, finally, God answered Job from the eye of a violent storm. He said "Why do you confuse the issue? Why do you talk without knowing what you're talking about? Pull yourself together, Job! Up on your feet! Stand tall! I have some questions for you, and I want some straight answers. Where were you when I created the earth? Tell me, since you know so much! Who decided on its size? Certainly you'll know that! Who came up with the blue prints and measurements? How was its foundation poured, and who set the cornerstone, while the morning stars sang in chorus and all the angels shouted praise? And who took charge of the ocean when it gushed forth like a baby from the womb? That was me! I wrapped it in soft clouds, and tucked it in safely at night. Then I made a*

playpen for it, a strong playpen so it couldn't run loose, And said, 'Stay here, this is your place. Your wild tantrums are confined to this place.'

God really does not need our input out to sort our problems. So why pray? Remember what Jesus said when his disciples asked how to pray; his reply was, "When you pray". Not 'if you pray'. (Luke 11 v1) Personally, I believe God does listen to and responds to our prayers. Prayer isn't about trying to get God to change his mind. It is about telling God what is important to us. Prayer also changes our minds & our attitudes. It gets us in line with his will and reminds us that that God's plans are the best ones. Can prayer persuade God to act? Surprising, as it may seem, God does respond to our prayers. It seems that God bases his priorities on what is important to us. When we tell him this is important to us, he will act. As someone once said 'It might be a coincidence that when I pray, things happen but all I know is when I stop praying the coincidences stop happening'. When we pray, we are building a two-way relationship with God. Yes, we should bring our concerns to God in prayer, but we really don't need to work out solutions, all we need to do is to praise him because his way of working is always to do the best for us. God answers prayer in one of three ways. He either gives us what we've asked for, gives us something else, or he changes our minds so we no longer want what we originally asked for. I am sure we can tell God our concerns in a non-asking way. I simply tell him the issues that are on my mind and thank him that he has solutions in place. No asking is needed.

When we pray about a problem our focus is on the problem. When we praise God for his ability to solve a problem out focus is on God. How heavy is a glass of water? Depends how long you hold it. The longer it's held, the heavier it becomes. It's the same with a problem, the longer it's held; the more it will weigh you down. Focusing on a problem, thinking about it, worrying about it is to keep hold of it. There was a pop song by The Wonder Stuff in 1991 with the words "I'm building up my problems to the size of a cow". When we keep hold of a problem, when we keep reminding God we need a solution, aren't we actually just doing that? Building up our problems to the size of a cow?

It doesn't have to be like this.

Chapter 2 But doesn't the Bible tell us to ask?

Matthew 7:7-9, 11-12
"Ask and it will be given to you; seek and you will find; knock and the door will be opened to you. For everyone who asks receives; the one who seeks finds; and to the one who knocks, the door will be opened. Which of you, if your son asks for bread, will give him a stone?
If you, then, though you are evil, know how to give good gifts to your children, how much more will your Father in heaven give good gifts to those who ask him!".

James 4:2-3
You desire but do not have, so you kill. You covet but you cannot get what you want, so you quarrel and fight. You do not have because you do not ask God.
When you ask, you do not receive, because you ask with wrong motives, that you may spend what you get on your pleasures.

Yes the Bible clearly does tell us to pray asking prayers. My argument is that so often ALL we do is ask. Prayer meetings are just endless repetition of shopping lists. According to James there is no point asking if our motives are wrong, as we won't get what we're asking for anyway.

Look at the Lord's Prayer. How much of it is asking? Very little. Look how much is asking & how much is praise. If we just used those proportions I believe we'd transform our prayer lives. The problem isn't that we shouldn't ask. The problem is that all we do is ask. We've got the balance wrong.

Only praying asking prayers can be like a person who only cleans their teeth on the day they have an appointment at the dentist. The dentist will know they haven't been cleaning their teeth regularly. Praying without asking means remembering that we don't have to wait until we have something to pray for. It means we pray anyway. It means we get into the habit of prayer. Look at Matthew 22:36-38

'Teacher, which is the greatest commandment in the Law?' Jesus replied: '"Love the Lord your God with all your heart and with all your soul and with all your mind." This is the first and greatest commandment.

How does endlessly asking, fit in with loving God with all your heart? The answer is that it doesn't. We don't make endless demands of the people we love and give nothing back.

When do you pray? When you have something to pray for? Prayer is so much more than telling God our shopping list. It's about developing a relationship. Our earthly relationships wouldn't get far if we only ever asked and never gave anything back or never even said 'Thank you'.

Every time we have a national disaster, people talk on the news about 'praying' for the victims. These are usually people who I've never heard mention God before nor do I hear them mention him again. Well, not until the next disaster. Nor do they mention him in any other context. I often wonder if God finds them as puzzling as I do. If I went along to your parents and asked them to give me money to buy a car I doubt I'd get very far. Yet people seem to think they can bring Almighty God out of cupboard and get him to perform and then put him back until the next time they have something they can't deal with. Can we honestly say we are we much better if in our prayers we are predominantly asking God? Jesus didn't squeeze prayer in to his life, he slotted it in. It was an important part of his life. Are we squeezers or slotters?

How easy is it to only thank and not ask? It should be very easy. Instead of worrying and working out the solutions we need, we can just thank God that he knows, that he cares and that he has everything under control. But we've been taught for so long that what prayer is, is the time we tell God our problems and ask him, or even worse demand, that he sort them out. We just need to ask, ask, ask. I'm challenging that. I'm saying we need to be thankful, to praise more than we ask and to put our focus on God, not on our problems.

So what does the Bible say?

Matthew 15:32-38
Jesus called his disciples to him and said, 'I

have compassion for these people; they have already been with me three days and have nothing to eat. I do not want to send them away hungry, or they may collapse on the way.'

His disciples answered, 'Where could we get enough bread in this remote place to feed such a crowd?'

'How many loaves do you have?' Jesus asked. 'Seven,' they replied, 'and a few small fish.'

He told the crowd to sit down on the ground.

Then he took the seven loaves and the fish, and when he had given thanks, he broke them and gave them to the disciples, and they in turn to the people.

They all ate and were satisfied. Afterwards the disciples picked up seven basketfuls of broken pieces that were left over.

The number of those who ate was four thousand men, besides women and children.

It isn't recorded if Jesus prayed anything else, only that he gave thanks. I suspect that many of us would be tempted to pray something like this poem

Heavenly Father bless us
And keep us all alive
There's ten of us for dinner
And not enough for five
Anon

But Jesus found that one small boy's lunch plus thankfulness equalled lunch for thousands.

Read what John says about this later.

John 6:23
Then some boats from Tiberias landed near the place where the people had eaten the bread after the Lord had given thanks. John is quite sure that the reason the miracle happened was because Jesus gave thanks. He thinks it's important enough to mention later on that not only had the people been fed but also that Jesus had given thanks. This tells me that giving thanks is powerful. When Jesus gave thanks over a small boy's lunch, it became enough to feed thousands. What would happen in our lives if we gave thanks more often?

Colossians 3:15 (The Message) *Let the peace of Christ keep you in tune with each other, in step with each other. None of this going off and doing your own thing. And cultivate thankfulness. Let the Word of Christ—the Message—have the run of the house. Give it plenty of room in your lives. Instruct and direct one another using good common sense. And sing, sing your hearts out to God! Let every detail in your lives—words, actions, whatever—be done in the name of the Master, Jesus, thanking God the Father every step of the way.* Cultivate thankfulness - surely a good way of cultivating thankfulness would be to praise instead of asking? I've used the translation from The Message because the word cultivate fits so well. Cultivation often starts with just planting a seed. I once bought some raspberry canes by mail order. Ten dead sticks arrived. My husband reluctantly agreed to plant them anyway. Neither of us had much hope that any of them would grow. It's ok if your thanks starts off like seeds or my raspberry canes. As unlikely as it seemed, all ten sticks sprouted & in a very short time began producing raspberries. Prayers full of thanks will blossom & produce fruit too. It's not important to be able to pray lovely flowery prayers. It isn't the words that God hears; it's the way they're spoken. Attitude is what counts. And it's quite impossible to shriek at God while praising him for what he's done. My approach to God is more like Isaiah:

Isaiah 6:1-5
In the year that King Uzziah died, I saw the Lord, high and exalted, seated on a throne; and the train of his robe filled the temple.
Above him were seraphim, each with six wings: with two wings they covered their faces, with two they covered their feet, and with two they were flying. And they were calling to one another:
'Holy, holy, holy is the Lord Almighty; the whole earth is full of his glory.'
At the sound of their voices the doorposts and thresholds shook and the temple was filled with smoke.
'Woe to me!' I cried. 'I am ruined! For I am a man of unclean lips, and I live among a people of unclean lips, and my eyes have seen the King, the Lord Almighty.'

Isaiah saw God and didn't say "Wow, get me; I must be super spiritual if God has appeared to me". Instead, he became aware of his own sinfulness and need of forgiveness. Like Isaiah, being close to God should make us humble, not arrogant. The more I think about what God has done for me the more thankful I become and the need to ask for anything begins to fade away. Twice a month I spend my Saturday evenings praying at Nightchurch, a city centre church that is open for clubbers from 9.30pm until 2am. We have worship, a prayer room, a quiet area, people to talk to, candles to light and a café. It takes church to where the people are. Someone recently came into the prayer room and asked us what our expectations are at the start of the evening and if we ever go home disappointed. I explained that for me, I don't turn up with an agenda. I have already been blessed by God in my life and I don't go to Nightchurch for what I can get out of it but to praise him for what I have already received. I told her the story of how I was rescued by Deborah; a woman from my church, when the only home I had was a Women's Refuge. That was over 25 years ago but there is nothing Deborah can ever do to me that will stop me loving her for what she did. I don't love God to ensure I receive a constant stream of blessings. I don't need a constant feel good emotional fix. I don't need everything to always go my way to convince me God still loves me. I love God because he has already blessed me.

My journey
In 2006, we both had good jobs. We bought a brand new car. It wasn't something we'd done before but we needed to replace our 11 yr. old 7 seater car 4 wheel drive car. (we have 4

children) & as we go camping/caravanning a lot we find a 4wd useful. With few suitable secondhand cars on the market, we bought a new one. Soon after, we sold our house and bought a bigger one. Everything was great until my husband opted for redundancy. We assumed he would get another job. He didn't. Weeks later, my job came to an end too. I managed to find a series of temp jobs but they paid about half what I'd been earning before and bored me stiff. After a few months, I went along to a Youth for Christ prayer meeting.

A young man came up to me and said, "Don't hit me. I have a message from God for you that you're not going to like. God says will you please stop shouting at him. He knows your situation and he has everything in his hands. And if you will stop shouting, he says he will share with you one of his great truths". Far from wanting to hit him, I just laughed. I knew I had been shouting at God for months. I wanted him to tell me everything would be ok. I wanted a proper job. I wanted to provide for my family. I wanted a job that didn't make me want to cry with boredom. I thought long and hard about what the young man had said and resolved to try and stop shouting. I think it took me about 2 weeks. At that time, I was helping my son deliver the local free paper. It was another way of earning money and the exercise had to be good for me. As I delivered papers, God said to me:

"It's loving people".
"It's one of your great truths isn't it?"

"Yes. Not just one of them, but the greatest. It's not doing right or being right or even justice. Loving people is the only thing that matters".

Ephesians 3:20
Now to him who is able to do immeasurably more than all we ask or imagine, according to his power that is at work within us.

If God really can do more than we can ask or imagine why do we think we need to ask? Can we let go of our need to ask and just praise? Some people I have met have refused to even try. They tell me that the Bible instructs us to ask when we pray and they see no reason not to. I wonder if the real reason is that they have a need to tell God what they want, they don't quite trust him to act without instruction.
Or perhaps they want to claim 'x' happened because they prayed for it. Perhaps they want some of the credit. Or maybe they just need to feel important and that to leave everything in God's hands renders them powerless, unable even to tell God what they need and they just can't let go. Whatever the reason, they refuse to stop asking. Is this you?
If I gave a stone to one of my children they would know from the start that I hadn't given them bread. But 2,000 years ago bread wasn't ready sliced and in a plastic bag, it was an ash-covered lump, not dissimilar to a stone. For a moment, the child would think they'd got bread. Jesus promises that God will not do this to us.

Not for a moment will he pretend to give us something when we're really getting something else.

Or are you prepared to trust God enough to believe that he cares enough to make sure he sorts out your problems without being told?

Chapter 3 Do we really need to ask?

I'm going to start with a hard question. How often does God answer your prayers with exactly what you asked for? I doubt it's as often as you'd like. So another question - how often are your prayers answered in a way you didn't expect, by a person you never imagined could be involved, or answered in a far bigger way than you every dreamt of?

What about answers to prayers we haven't actually asked? Does God do stuff for us without being asked? The answer has to be 'Yes'. He put plans in place for us when we were still children, before we knew him. When we are following our own agenda, God still cares for us. Look at your life and remember times when God has done the unexpected for you. These are often the most desperate times, when we need prayer the most. Yet these are the times we don't need to pray because God has acted without being asked. I wonder what the balance is between how much God does that we haven't asked for compared to how much have?

What about times when we are too distraught to pray? Anyone who has been caught up in a seemingly impossible situation is likely to have experienced the helplessness of not knowing what to pray. The Bible tells us that in times like these God hears our hearts. In 1 Samuel, Hannah was so desperate for a baby she didn't have the words to say anymore. How many times had she prayed for a baby? Now she had given up using words. Praying in the temple her mouth moved but no words came out. The High Priest Eli assumed she was drunk. But God heard and answered her wordless prayer and gave her not only the son she longed for, but one who grew up to be the High Priest and prophet. But that wasn't all. Hannah got far more than she asked for. 1 Samuel 2 v 21 says this:

And the Lord was gracious to Hannah; she gave birth to three sons and two daughters. Meanwhile, the boy Samuel grew up in the presence of the Lord.

Hannah would have been content with just one child, but she ended up with six times as many children as she asked for. In 2012, we couldn't afford a family holiday. The next year I was really hoping for a miracle that would enable us to go away somewhere and have a break. I'd have been happy with a week's camping as long as it wasn't too cold and rainy. I just wanted time off from work and time to spend with my family. The short version is that we went to the Caribbean for a two-week stay in an all-inclusive resort. It was fabulous. It was an extravagant response to a request I hadn't actually made. God knew I wanted to go on holiday, I hadn't actually asked. But it was more than I ever expected. It was far more than I ever would have asked for, even if I were still asking. Even more unbelievable, after we returned home, the travel company sent us a huge refund. Other holidaymakers had complained about overcrowding at the hotel & we were all given a substantial refund. I'd had a great time; ok the pool was often overcrowded so I had to swim in the Caribbean Sea, which wasn't exactly a hardship for someone like me who loves sand and sea. I used to take a roll from the breakfast buffet and feed the gorgeous tropical fish as I swam. Yes, there had been a lot of pushing and shoving in the buffet restaurant but we had never been unable to find a table nor had we ever found the food had all gone. I can't say anything had spoilt my holiday. For us, it was an extravagant gift from the God who loves us.

This wasn't a one off occurrence. The previous year, one of my daughters' asked me to look out for a car for her as she was taking her driving test in a few weeks. A friend rang up out of the blue and asked if we knew anyone who would be interested in a small car. It was a perfect starter car for a bargain price so I snapped it up, parking it at my eldest daughter's house until her sister passed her test. The morning after the car arrived, my eldest daughter's car failed the MOT big time. She couldn't afford to get it repaired, but didn't have to worry immediately as a great replacement car was sitting on her drive! All she had to do was to change the insurance over, which was simple enough and didn't cost any more as the cars were very similar. By the time her sister had passed her driving test, the original car was fixed. We didn't ask God to do

this. We didn't know the car would spectacularly fail the MOT but God did and made provision. We were probably praying that her car would pass the MOT, we certainly weren't praying for the solution we got. On my usual praise walk past the school one morning I spotted a mobile phone lying on the pavement. I picked it up but couldn't turn it on. That wasn't surprising given that it had rained steadily all night. I took the phone home, hoping to dry it out enough to try & identify the owner. Back home, I opened the phone & took the battery out. The phone was wet inside so I towel dried it carefully and left it in pieces hoping it would dry out. When I put it back together, I was pleased when the phone showed signs of life. I scrolled through the contacts and noticed a name I knew - someone who had been a member of the school PTA when my youngest children attended the school. I decided to hand the phone into the school and hoped they would find the owner. I drove to the school on my way to work. As I parked in a side street, the phone began to ring, so I answered it. The caller was quite bemused. I explained that I'd found the phone earlier and was just bringing it back to drop it off now the school was open.
The caller agreed I should do that but I got the feeling she didn't quite believe me. If she'd believed me when I told her that I was right by the school, she would have said that she would wait outside the school for me. But she didn't. As I walked past the parents standing around the school gate, I heard one mum say to another "I'm really glad you rang it when you did". I

turned to the speaker and held out her phone. She was pleased to get it back. She thought she might have dropped it after attending a PTA meeting. Standing outside the school she asked her friend to ring the phone in the hope of finding it. That would not have helped had the phone still been lying wet on the pavement or kicked into the hedgerow by children running into the playground as the phone was too wet to respond. If the owner is a Christian, (or even if she wasn't!) she may have been praying that her phone was outside the school and undamaged. I doubt she was praying that her phone had been rescued, dried out and would arrive back at the school at the same time she was there to drop her children off. Isn't it a waste of time when we try and work out our own solutions? So why do we bother?

As I write this book, one of my Grandsons had a fall & his teeth went through his lip. Rushed off to A&E with his distraught mum, she was amazed when while he as being assessed by a nurse, a doctor walked over, looked at the injury and declared that it didn't need stitches but would heal quickly with just salt water rinses. The nurse assured my daughter that the doctor was in fact their facial injury specialist. And he was right, it healed up without stitches. I wasn't praying when he was rushed off to hospital. I was away on a camping trip with my phone switched off. I didn't even know he'd had a fall. But it didn't matter. God knew. I wasn't surprised that God provided a specialist to treat my Grandson without being asked.

My parents were abusive and inevitably I was left with a lot of anger against them. During a phone conversation with my Auntie, she said that she thought God wanted to be my parent. The first time she said this it made me really angry. It sounded so unlikely and was nothing more than a trite statement. As if I should start saying that God was my special parent & have a nice warm feeling. I didn't need some pseudo religious feeling. I needed something real. I needed a parent. Only people without parents will understand the huge gap their absence leaves in a person's life. The second time she said it I was just as angry but this time she told me to ask God for an explanation. So I went into the kitchen & asked God to explain what Auntie meant. The response came quickly. God said this - "I want you to think of a time when you needed a parent and there was no one there to help you". And then he shouted, "Don't bother. You'll never find a time when you needed someone and there was no one there to help.
I know your parents are useless but I always ensure there is someone there to replace them". I was stunned. But I just knew that even if I tried I'd never find a time that I'd been left parent less. I'm not sure it had ever occurred to me that God did stuff like this. What I am sure is that I never asked God to do it. But he did it anyway. The more I thought about it, the more incidences I remembered when I needed someone and sure enough, someone was there. Like so many
other abused children, I married a man who treated me in just the same way as had my

parents. He was violent and constantly undermined me, ensuring I had little self-esteem. I left him & packed my two daughters and a few of our possessions into my car ready to move into a Women's Refuge. I didn't have anywhere else to go. With my car all packed, I stopped off to help run the church Brownie pack which I'd recently started doing every Wednesday. The pack was run by Deborah, I mentioned to her that I wouldn't be living at home anymore. She insisted that I move into her flat. She lived in a tiny one bedroom flat in a tower block. I didn't know her very well and didn't want to put anyone out that much. She made me promise to ring and tell her the next day if the refuge was ok. The refuge was grim and it was miles away from the girls' school and my job. The next night, I rang Deborah as agreed and admitted the refuge was awful. It would have been easy for her to ignore my plight and given that she'd had 24 hours to think about her rash offer, she could have backtracked. But she didn't. She had a tiny flat. There really wasn't room for an extra adult let alone an adult with two children. She could have decided that someone else would be better placed to help out. That we weren't her responsibility. But she didn't ignore us. She took us in, just the way a parent should. The girls slept in her bed while Deborah & I slept on a bed settee in the lounge. We stayed in her flat until the court ordered my husband leave our flat so I could move back in. It was exactly the kind of situation when a parent would help out. God gave me Deborah. It had never occurred to me to ask God to provide someone to help me. It wasn't something I'd specifically prayed for. After all, I'd been praying for a space in a Women's Refuge. But God delivered a much better result without being asked.

Deborah came to the rescue again some months later when I was taken ill. Deborah and I had taken our Brownie pack away for the weekend. I was taken off to hospital leaving my daughters in Deborah's care. She moved into my flat so she could look after them. I've no idea how she juggled getting them to school while carrying on with her own teaching job but she did. I was in a hospital out in the countryside, quite a way from home. Deborah didn't drive so she commandeered people to collect her and the girls and bring them to see me. Every evening. As she said, it was really important that the girls saw their Mum everyday. It certainly was. One of my girls gave me a 'Get Well' card. Inside she'd written, "Dear Mum please don't die"! God put the people in place to be there for me. Without being asked.

After my conversations with Auntie and God, I began to expect God to put people in place to help me out. I never asked for them, I simply expected them to be there and they always were. Like the time I wanted to go away to a conference. My husband was working nights & couldn't take time off to look after our 2 small children, as his holidays were mainly restricted to factory shutdown times. I told my story to a friend at church and said that I knew God had someone ready to be replacement parents and help me out. Her reply was that she would be honoured to be God's chosen replacement and was very happy to take care of my children. My husband dropped them off at her house every evening and they slept there. I'm not actually sure how much sleep any of them got, with my two and her three but I know a lot of fun was had by all. This is the God who is able to do more than we can ask or think. Why do we hang on to needing to pray asking prayers?

I've never been one if those people who pray before every journey. One day, I was driving my two youngest children home from school. I was doing the speed limit on an urban road when I went to pull out to overtake a parked car. As I tried to turn the steering wheel, I felt a hand hold my elbow, preventing me from turning the wheel. Suddenly, a car overtook me. Had I pulled out, I would have collided with the speeding car. I managed to avoid the parked car, feeling immensely relieved that although I had failed to notice the car about to overtake me, the other overtaker had failed to notice both the speed limit and failed to notice that I was about to overtake a parked car, God was looking out for me and my children. Without me ever asking him to do that. If I had said a special prayer before setting off, would God have taken better care of us? Hardly. We escaped a potentially serious accident and the kids did not even notice. And, yes, I said 'Thank you'.

So is there any point in spending time asking God to do this or that? Is there any benefit in

becoming stressed and anxious either when God answers prayers without being asked? Remember the glass of water that becomes heavier the longer it is held? Can we put our problems down and leave them there?
Can we put our trust in God and believe that he knows what we want before we ask?

Matthew 7: 11-12
If you, then, though you are evil, know how to give good gifts to your children, how much more will your Father in heaven give good gifts to those who ask him!

Those of us who are parents probably don't find it difficult to know what our children want. For my daughter's 2nd birthday, I bought her a small trike. She immediately sat on it and announced, "Here it is what I wanted". She didn't have the language skills to tell me she wanted a trike. She probably didn't even know that a trike was more suitable for her than a bike. All she knew was that when she saw local kids whizzing round on bikes, she wanted to join them. Well over 30 years later, I still remember the joy I experienced from giving a toddler a present she really really wanted. As her parent, I want her to give her good things and it gave me pleasure to see her enjoyment of that little trike.
Much more recently, my son passed his driving test and with the help of Granny, we bought him a small car. 15 months later, my car had to be scrapped as it was beyond economic repair. My son suggested that instead of me buying a

replacement car, I should lend him the money to buy a better car and keep his small one. To be honest, it wasn't the most attractive suggestion, but I understood that fitting his 6ft frame into the small car was not comfortable and so he got an upgrade and I drive around in a dinky car. But I know how much he enjoys driving his new car. Do we really believe that God does not know what is best for us?

So if we're not asking God for stuff, what should we be saying? Easy. Let's just thank God and praise him. A friend of mine asked me to prayer walk around the school where she works. So I started doing it at least 5 days a week. I used to get up and pray for half an hour every morning so I just started taking the dog for a walk instead and praying while we walked. After about 3 months, God said to me. "You know you say the same prayers every day. Why don't you junk them all and just praise? ". So I did. 30 minutes of saying thank you to God. I admit, it was hard to begin with. When I feel really concerned about something, all I can do is say 'Thank you God that you'll sort this for me!'

No one is problem free. Just because I'm a Christian, doesn't mean I don't have problems. I will say this – that just thanking God somehow changed my attitudes. Imagine starting the day with 30 minutes of positive thinking. Concentrating on what is good, what I'm grateful for has changed how I approach the rest of the day.

Chapter 4
So what if we prayed without asking?

Philippians 4:6 The Message

Don't fret or worry. Instead of worrying, pray. Let petitions and praises shape your worries into prayers, letting God know your concerns. Before you know it, a sense of God's wholeness, everything coming together for good, will come and settle you down. It's wonderful what happens when Christ displaces worry at the centre of your life.

Paul perfectly sums up what this book is about. Letting petitions and praises shape our worries into prayers. Bringing our worries to God is not the same as battering God with demands or insisting on our own solutions. Instead, we should be bringing our concerns to God and praising him that he already has a solution in place.

In 2 Chronicles, three kings ganged up and declared war on Israel.

2 Chronicles 20 v1-9 The Message
Some time later the Moabites and Ammonites, accompanied by Meunites, joined forces to

make war on Jehoshaphat. Jehoshaphat received this intelligence report: "A huge force is on its way from beyond the Dead Sea to fight you. There'sno time to waste—they're already at Hazazon Tamar, the oasis of En Gedi."

Shaken, Jehoshaphat prayed. He went to God for help and ordered a nationwide fast. The country of Judah united in seeking God's help—they came from all the cities of Judah to pray to God.Then Jehoshaphat took a position before the assembled people of Judah and Jerusalem at The Temple of God in front of the new courtyard and said, "O God, God of our ancestors, are you not God in heaven above and ruler of all kingdoms below? You hold all power and might in your fist—no one stands a chance against you! And didn't you make the natives of this land leave as you brought your people Israel in, turning it over permanently to your people Israel, the descendants of Abraham your friend? They have lived here and built a holy house of worship to honour you, saying, 'When the worst happens—whether war or flood or disease or famine—and we take our place before this Temple (we know you are personally present in this place!) and pray out our pain and trouble, we know that you will listen and give victory.'

Three neighbouring kings gang up and threaten Israel. King Jehoshaphat's response isn't to beg God to send him help. He doesn't start to tell God the solution he wants. He doesn't even complain that it's going to make God look bad if Israel are crushed by the other tribes. Instead he calls the people together to publicly praise

God and then to bring his concerns to God. But his praises come first. And he doesn't have a readymade solution that he wants God to deliver. He praises God for past victories and simply says 'we know that you will listen and give victory'. God's response to Jehoshaphat is swift. No sooner had Jehoshaphat stopped speaking when a prophet brought God's response:

2 Chronicles 20 v 15. The Message

Don't be afraid; don't pay any mind to this vandal horde. This is God's war, not yours. Tomorrow you'll go after them; see, they're already on their way up the slopes of Ziz; you'll meet them at the end of the ravine near the wilderness of Jeruel. You won't have to lift a hand in this battle; just stand firm, Judah and Jerusalem, and watch God's saving work for you take shape. Don't be afraid, don't waver. March out boldly tomorrow— God is with you."

This is God's war, not yours. That is the key. The battle is not ours. The battle is God's. The big question is, do we trust God enough to leave him to sort out our problems and concerns? Jehoshaphat did. He put his faith in God to deal with the problem:

2 Chronicles 20 v 21-24 The Message

After talking it over with the people, Jehoshaphat appointed a choir for God; dressed in holy robes, they were to march ahead of the troops, singing,

Give thanks to God,   His love never quits.
As soon as they started shouting and praising, God set ambushes against the men of Ammon, Moab, and Mount Seir as they were attacking Judah, and they all ended up dead. The Ammonites and Moabites mistakenly attacked those from Mount Seir and massacred them. Then, further confused, they went at each other, and all ended up killed.

Praying without asking certainly worked for Jehoshaphat. I suspect that wasn't the first time he had trusted God. Jehoshaphat had already found that when God is all we have that's when we find that God is all we need.

My journey towards praying without asking began with this event some years ago. One March, I returned home from holiday to be told that one of my closest friends, was ill in hospital with a twisted bowel. I didn't know what that was or how serious so I rang another friend who's a nurse. '"I'm sorry" she said. "It means
her bowel has burst. She will either die from septicemia or from shock as they open her up and try and repair the damage. Either way she is unlikely to last the night". She was just 39 years old and mum to two young children. "All we can do is put drains in & start praying" my nurse friend told me. "The hospital has done the first"; I said "And we'll do the second". As a church group we started praying. One woman set her alarm for every hour and woke up to say a prayer. I got up early and prayed for a couple of hours. This was before I learnt to pray without

asking so I specifically asked that she survive perfectly – without a bag. What 39 year old wants a bag? I wanted a complete healing. At 8am our vicar went into the hospital. He didn't realise how ill she was and was surprised to find her on life support. But she was still alive. She opened her eyes and to the consternation of the nurse said '" I feel so much better. That terrible pain has gone". "In that case"; said the nurse; "We'll try and put you back together". She went back down to theatre for a second operation. She survived, but her recovery was slow. We carried on praying. Some of began to wonder what God was doing. Alive, but unable to eat real food, living on liquids and too ill to leave hospital.

Outside the school one morning I said to the vicar. "I know what you're going to do. You're going to raise her from the dead. Don't go without me". He admitted he thought that she was likely to die and yes, he would try & get in to and raise her from the dead. Another Mum saw me talking to him. "I know what you're plotting," she said. "You think you'll have to raise her from the dead. Well you're not going without me!"

The 3 of us were praying that we didn't have to do it. But it made us examine our faith. Do we believe that God can and does raise people from the dead? Absolutely. Do we believe that God would raise someone because we asked? Hmmm. Not quite so sure. You know what? The three of us got to the point where we knew we had enough faith to try.

In May, her Mum rang me and asked me to go to

the hospital to visit. I'd been 2 days before, but her mum was insistent I should go today. Our church was due to have a meal together that evening so I dropped my kids off & went to the hospital. I quickly realised why her Mum had wanted me to go. She was barely alive. She was so dehydrated her skin had sunk between the bones of her fingers. She looked like a skeleton. I knew she was just fading away. I've never seen anyone die but I knew what I was looking at. I read this to her:

2 Corinthians 6 v 9
We live close to death, but here we are still alive, we have been beaten within an inch of our lives. Our hearts ache but we always have joy.
We are poor but we give spiritual riches to others. We own nothing but we have everything.

I went back to where the church were meeting and said we needed to pray. Someone said "This isn't a time to just all hold hands and say a little prayer. In Acts they prayed all night. We should give up something. Let's pray all night".
My husband was on the night shift so everyone came to my house.
Acts 12 v 5-16 The Message

All the time that Peter was under heavy guard in the jailhouse, the church prayed for him most strenuously.
Then the time came for Herod to bring him out for the kill. That night, even though shackled to two soldiers, one on either side, Peter slept like

a baby. And there were guards at the door keeping their eyes on the place. Herod was taking no chances!

Suddenly there was an angel at his side and light flooding the room. The angel shook Peter and got him up: "Hurry!" The handcuffs fell off his wrists. The angel said, "Get dressed. Put on your shoes." Peter did it. Then, "Grab your coat and let's get out of here." Peter followed him, but didn't believe it was really an angel—he thought he was dreaming.

Past the first guard and then the second, they came to the iron gate that led into the city. It swung open before them on its own, and they were out on the street, free as the breeze. At the first intersection the angel left him, going his own way. That's when Peter realized it was no dream. "I can't believe it—this really happened! The Master sent his angel and rescued me from Herod's vicious little production and the spectacle the Jewish mob was looking forward to."

Still shaking his head, amazed, he went to Mary's house, the Mary who was John Mark's mother. The house was packed with praying friends. When he knocked on the door to the courtyard, a young woman named Rhoda came to see who it was. But when she recognized his voice—Peter's voice!—she was so excited and eager to tell everyone Peter was there that she forgot to open the door and left him standing in the street.

But they wouldn't believe her, dismissing her, dismissing her report. "You're crazy," they said.

She stuck by her story, insisting. They still wouldn't believe her and said, "It must be his angel." All this time poor Peter was standing out in the street, knocking away.

Peter had been imprisoned and was due to be executed the following day. The church prayed all night. When there was a knock at the door, they didn't think it would be Peter and indeed the girl sent to open the door was so astonished, that she didn't open it, but rushed back to the room to tell the others instead! They told her she must be out of her mind. Yet they had met up to pray, presumably for Peter's release. When it happened they couldn't believe it. We don't need to be 100% confident before
we pray. We don't pray because we have great faith; we have great faith because we pray. I find it interesting that Peter is described as 'sleeping like a baby', I'm not sure I would be if I knew I was due to be executed the next day.

Were we 100% confident at the start of the night? I don't think so. But we had run out of options. It seemed the hospital could do no more for our friend. Like Jehoshaphat we found that when God is all we have, God is all we need. We prayed. We thanked God because we knew that he could heal. We thanked him that so many people cared that she should live. We didn't shout and scream at God. We'd been praying for her for three months. We'd said everything there was to say so we just thanked God that he had heard our prayers. We read theBible. We heard God speak. We were rubbish and fell asleep at 2am. But those 3 ½ hours were an amazing time. We gave up sleep to spend time with God and he turned up. I don't think we were surprised when the next day her mum phoned to say that at 2am, my friend had sat up and asked for tea and toast – the first food she had eaten for 3 months. While we were praying, the hospital had realised that she had contracted MRSA and moved her into a private room. Even they were astonished at her recovery.

The consultant told her that she was the only one of his patients to have a twisted bowel & leave that hospital without a bag. She has no ongoing effects from the MRSA, despite contracting it when malnourished and dehydrated. Despite only have one metre of bowel instead of seven metres, her digestive system works perfectly. She knows she was given her life back and despite being very shy, became a street pastor. As for the group that prayed that night, we were never the same again. We gave God our time. Look what he did with it. And it's always true.

I started thanking and not asking one January. My daughter who lives 200 miles away was expecting a baby the following March. She texted early one Thursday morning to say her waters had broken. We couldn't rush straight off to be with her. I'd started a new job the previous week & my husband only had a temp job. Taking time off wasn't an option for either of us. We waited for news all day Thursday and then all day Friday. We'd arranged to stay at her in laws when the baby arrived and on Friday, her mother in law rang me and asked us to drive down as soon as we could as the baby would have to arrive soon and she was feeling stressed and wanted some support. We left straight after work and drove down, getting intermittent updates. I became increasingly concerned, not just for mum & baby but I really didn't want her to have a C-section. The couple lived in a 3rd floor flat. It would be really difficult for her to climb up 3 flights of stairs carrying a baby & maybe a buggy. She drives, but he doesn't so having a C-section could imprison her in the flat for 6 weeks until she was allowed to drive again. I really didn't want her to have a C-section. But I couldn't ask! Instead I thanked God that he understood my concerns and could be trusted to look after my daughter and baby. We sat waiting with the in laws until 3am. They'd been no news since before midnight. At 3am I decided we should go to bed and fell asleep immediately. I felt really really peaceful which is surprising given the circumstances. At 4.45am we were awoken by the phone ringing. The decision had been taken to deliver baby by C-section but when my daughter arrived in the theatre, the doctor decided to try a ventouse instead & baby arrived. No need for a C-section after all. And it all happened just before 3am. I didn't tell God what to do. I didn't even ask politely. I simply trusted God and he took care of my daughter and Grandson just as I wanted him to. The question is, would I have got a better result if I'd asked? If I begged God all the way down the motorway?

I can't see there was a better result. Mum and baby safe and well without need for a C section I didn't want anything else. I never expected to see my Grandson on the day he was born, but his delayed arrival meant that I did and that was really special to me.

Not so traumatic, but this next incident was still potentially distressing. My eldest daughter and her family went away for the weekend leaving their terrier, Millie, in my care. Millie is well used to spending time at our house so I was astonished when I opened my front door and she legged it. I could only gaze in horror as she ran down the road at breakneck speed. I picked up her lead & went after her. My neighbour shouted, "You need to run faster than that if youwant to catch that dog". It wasn't the most helpful thing to say. At the end of the road I took a guess that Millie had stayed on the same side of the road and turned left. I hoped she would just keep following the pavement and that I'd find her eventually. I wasn't sure how long it would take for a terrier to get tired but suspected it might take her longer than it would take me. Walking along, it was unbearable that I might have to tell my small Grandsons that I'd lost their dog. They are too small to remember life without Millie. I didn't want them to start now. I couldn't

ask, I could only praise God that he knew the trouble I was in. "'Don't fret" said Paul. Don't fret! I'd lost a dog I was looking after. I asked everyone I saw if they had seen a small dog running loose but no one had. At the next junction I turned left again. As I turned, I saw my friend Debbie just going through her back gate with her dog. I called out to her & asked if she'd seen a small dog. She shouted back "One called Millie?" Yes. One called Millie. She called her husband; Ken and he came out of the garden with Millie in his arms. Apparently, Millie had stopped to say hello to their dog and they'd noticed that Millie didn't seem to have anyone with her but she did have a tag with her name and a phone number so they decided to take her home and ring the number. That wouldn't have worked, as the family were away. Did I need to walk the streets begging God to help me find Millie? Would it have made any difference if I had? God knew I needed help to get Millie back and he put Debbie, Ken and Lucky in just the right place at exactly the right time to provide that help. Millie pulled a similar stunt a few weeks later. We'd had a grand family day out to celebrate my eldest daughter's birthday. My middle daughter & her family had come up for the weekend and we all went for a picnic on the beach before going back to my daughter's house for birthday cake. I got there first and let Millie back into the house. I was just putting candles on the cake when I heard a key in the door. I knew there was a risk Millie might leg it again if the front door was opened as her family were not at home but presumed that it must be my eldest daughter, her sister doesn't have a key. I didn't know she'd given her sister a key. Millie panicked when her family still were not home and dashed out the door and disappeared. With my son in law I, started walking the streets searching for Millie. I went to the park, but no one had seen her. Eventually, I got in my car & started driving round the streets. I didn't find Millie. I did meet up with my eldest daughter and her family returning home from the picnic. I wound my window down and admitted I'd lost Millie. Again. She laughed and said, "We know". She went on to explain that she'd had a phone call from some teenage boys saying they'd found her dog. She could not imagine how Millie had escaped from the secure area of the garden but drove to where the boys were and collected Millie feeling relieved that after Millie's previous escape bid she'd bought a new tag engraved with her mobile phone number. Millie had run about a mile and was much further away than I had ever imagined she would be. Once again, God had answered my unspoken prayers. He knew I needed to find Millie. I didn't need to ask.

Paul wrote this in 1 Thessalonians 5:18

Give thanks in all circumstances; for this is God's will for you in Christ Jesus.

Hmmm all circumstances. Not just the good ones. But Paul didn't just tell us to praise God in all circumstances, according to Acts he took his own advice.

Acts 16 v 22-26 NIV

The crowd joined in the attack against Paul and

Silas, and the magistrates ordered them to be stripped and beaten with rods. After they had been severely flogged, they were thrown into prison, and the jailer was commanded to guard them carefully. When he received these orders, he put them in the inner cell and fastened their feet in the stocks. About midnight Paul and Silas were praying and singing hymns to God, and the other prisoners were listening to them. Suddenly there was such a violent earthquake

that the foundations of the prison were shaken. At once all the prison doors flew open, and everyone's chains came loose.

Paul and Silas were praying and singing. I'm not sure I would feel like singing after being beaten and then imprisoned, but they did. I can't see complaining prayers going alongside singing either. In an awful situation, injured and chained up in a windowless cell, Paul and Silas didn't focus on the awfulness of their situation. They just praised. The result - an earthquake.

Chapter 5 How to pray

Eph 3 v 12 NIV

In him (Jesus Christ) and through faith in him we may approach God with freedom and confidence.

So if we're not asking, how do we pray? How about starting with the Lord's Prayer and using that as a template?

Luke 11 v 1-4

One day Jesus was praying in a certain place. When he finished, one of his disciples said to him, 'Lord, teach us to pray, just as John taught his disciples.'
He said to them, 'When you pray, say:
"Father, hallowed be your name, your kingdom come.
Give us each day our daily bread.
Forgive us our sins, for we also forgive everyone who sins against us. And lead us not into temptation."'

Of course we should be bringing our concerns to God. But we don't have to do it by asking. When

I want to pray about something I say "God I want to bring x before you. You already know my concerns. I thank and praise you that you have a solution already in place. What could be simpler? I don't need a specific form of words. There isn't a formula that will unlock heaven and persuade God to act. This isn't an incantation. It's just praising God for who he is and thanking him for what he has done in the past.

Who should we be praying to – God or Jesus? Jesus clearly told us we can pray directly to God. The prayer he taught us starts 'Our Father'. More importantly, the Greek word we've translated as 'father' would be better translated as 'daddy'. This isn't a formal relationship; it's an intimate one. Jesus told his disciples to pray in his name. In his first letter to Timothy, Paul says:

1 Timothy 2 v 5 NIV

There's one God and only one, and one Priest-Mediator between God and us – Jesus, who offered himself in exchange for everyone held captive by sin, to set them all free.

Apparently, Marie Antoinette complained to her mother about the protocol of the French court.
She claimed it was so formal that the woman who was responsible for taking Marie Antoinette's clothes out of the wardrobe, was not important enough to hand them to the Queen of France so, the clothes would be passed to her via several women of increasing importance, but in the meantime, Marie got cold waiting for her clothes to arrive. We don't have any such

problems in approaching God. Through Jesus, we have the right to come straight into the presence of God and talk to him directly. We have no need of an intermediary.

But what to say? If we're used to spending our prayer time telling God our problems and the solutions we think we need, how do we fill that space? The easiest way is to use words from the Bible. Praise God using his many names, Almighty God, Everlasting Father, I Am. Praise Jesus using the words used to describe him - Wonderful Counsellor, Prince of Peace, Saviour, Redeemer. Use psalms or praise songs. Praise him for all the good things in your life. I find these prayers really powerful as they change me. Instead of thinking of all my problems, in order to praise God for the good things in my life I actually have to think what they are. When I do that I automatically feel more cheerful and praise becomes easier. The more cheerful I become, the easier it is to think of things to praise God for. The more I praise, the more cheerful I become. I expect you get the picture. The things I praise God for aren't usually things.

They're much more likely to be people and relationships. Psalm 136 is a good place to start as is Mary's song of praise, the Magnificat in Luke 1 46-55

I also recommend speaking out loud. There is something powerful about the spoken word. Yes, you're likely to feel self-conscious speaking out loud when there's no one there, or even worse if there is someone who can hear you. But when you are alone, speak. It doesn't have to be loud, a whisper is fine. When I first started prayer walking, I used to put a scarf over my mouth so I had something to mumble into and no one would see my lips moving. I'm not so self-conscious now and talk quietly as I walk along. I don't know if anyone notices. Maybe they think I am talking to my dog, or maybe I am singing (I often am). Funnily enough, talking to yourself is viewed as odd, but singing to yourself is absolutely fine!

The most important prayer to pray is this "Your will be done". When we pray this, we do two things. One, we acknowledge the sovereignty of God and two, we pass responsibility for situations onto God, rather than thinking we can solve them ourselves. If we get stuck for something to say, we can rely on the Holy Spirit to help us out:

Romans 8 26-28 NIV
God's Spirit is right alongside helping us along. If we don't know how or what to pray, it doesn't matter. He does our praying in and for us, making prayer out of our wordless sighs, our aching groans. He knows us far better than we know ourselves, knows our pregnant condition, and keeps us present before God. That's why we can be so sure that every detail in our lives of love for God is worked into something good.

Wordless sighs and aching groans are more powerful prayers than empty words. I do try to avoid telling God what I want him to do, mainly because I'm not always sure what the solution should be and often even when I think I know, I'm actually wrong. I have a friend who suffered with asthma for years, which was treated with asthma medication. Until the day he was given an ECG and the doctor found out he has a heart condition. Now on the right medication, he doesn't suffer from asthma. I know God could sort out his heart condition even if someone prayed for him to be healed of asthma, but why complicate matters? When you pray, just change the words round. Every time you want to say 'ask' say 'thank'. This is what I could have prayed for my daughter and what I did pray:

Father God I thank and praise you that you are an almighty and all powerful God. You know how concerned I am about my daughter and her baby. So I'm ~~asking you to take~~ I'm thanking you for taking care of her. You know her flat is on the 3rd floor and her husband can't drive so I'm ~~asking you to make sure she doesn't get a C-section.~~ I just want to thank you that you love her even more than I do and I praise you because I know that you will take care of her. It's just a case of switching our words and keeping the focus on God's ability to solve the issue rather than on the problem itself.

To praise God in our prayers carries the requirement that we are thankful. We can't be half hearted about this. We need at the very least to want to be thankful and that is not always easy. In fact it may be the hardest part. What we need to do is to shift the focus of our

prayers away from us. When the focus of our prayers is on us, we are most likely to be focusing on our problems. Thinking about someone else means we aren't thinking about ourselves. Focusing on God enables us to become more thankful. If you find shifting the focus too difficult, then shift it from focusing on your problems to focusing on what you have to be thankful for. The risk is that it is easy to slip from thinking about reasons to be thankful to thinking about our problems again, but apply a bit of discipline and every time your mind wanders to your problems, pull it back again to focus on your blessings. I do recommend keeping a journal. Write in it everything that you have found to praise God for. Add all the worries and concerns that you have brought to God. Make sure you include all the problems that you thought were not possible to resolve until you
God sorted them anyway. Or keep a jar and on slips of paper, write all the problems that God has answered without being asked. Pop the slips in the jar and watch them mount up. If you feel discouraged, reread your journal or read those slips. Since I've been praising and not asking, my daughter decided she wanted to buy a house rather than to spend a lot of money on renting. It made more sense to buy one, but while she could afford to pay a mortgage, she didn't have enough for a deposit. We couldn't afford to lend her that much money. I could not see how she was ever going to be able to buy her own house. As I write, she's just texted to say she's made an

offer on a house she wants to buy. She can do this, because, miraculously, someone has provided the amount needed for a deposit. I didn't worry or fret, I just passed it over to God.
I'd like to tell you that you'll be able to seamlessly move from asking prayers to thanking prayers but I can't. It won't be seamless. It's likely to be stuttery, difficult, maybe one step forward and two steps back sometimes. But I know it is possible. I know, because I have done it and I keep trying to do it. I keep hoping that one day I won't slip back, but at the moment I still struggle when there are difficulties in my life that God could so easily solve but doesn't and there is nothing for me to do but accept that God is seeing a bigger picture. I still get disappointed, frustrated and annoyed. To praise God always, does require us to empty our hearts of desire and fill them with unwavering belief that God loves us and has always done the best for us, is doing the best for us and will continue to do the best for us. We don't need to ask God anything. We don't need to remind him what we need. We don't have to waste any time thinking up solutions. We only need to trust God. Imagine you have a problem with a work colleague and it's causing you problems. Perhaps your boss makes unrealistic demands, or a colleague keeps letting you down or doesn't pull their weight. Maybe you're being bullied & the management are turning a blind eye. I've had all these problems. So the easy prayer is "God get this person moved away from me or get me another job". But the thankful

prayer is "God you know this situation and you have own solution". Maybe God wants to use this situation to teach us something. When I am in difficult situations I do mention to God that I'm struggling. I'm not suggesting that our problems become the elephant in the room that no one dares mention. As I write this, I have just been transferred to a new department and have a rather demanding boss who seems to expect me to work well beyond my pay grade, work longer than my contracted hours without extra pay and produce complex pieces of work within ludicrously short timescales. He keeps telling me that if I show I can do work above my pay grade, I will become eligible for promotion. I've been working here in a low-grade job for 4 ½ years and haven't seen a promotion opportunity yet. His words are wearing thin. He's just told me to design a logo for the project we're working on. And quickly. I looked up to heaven & said can't I just have a new job? Maybe if I had lots of time and a clear head I could design a logo but right now? No. Then an idea popped into my head. "Google it for inspiration". So I did. Sometimes it's just not necessary to reinvent the wheel.

I met Isabella through my involvement in politics. She suffers from a serious illness but it doesn't stop her from holding down a job and being politically active. She was admitted to hospital and didn't seem to be getting better. I had only met her a couple of times but I knew she was a Christian and I really wanted to go and pray with her. But she was in hospital in London and I live 200 miles away. Then I was offered a job interview in London. So I had my train fare paid and I had an afternoon free. I messaged her and arranged to visit. She had now been in hospital for three weeks. I knew she was ill, but I was shocked when I saw her. Lying in bed, she barely even opened her eyes when I went into her room. I'd bought her some luxury Belgian chocolates from a shop on Oxford Street, (my interview had been for a job in Brussels so it seemed appropriate to buy her Belgian chocolates). But she never looked at them so I put them on the side. She did tell me the doctors were now saying they were considering putting her on the transplant list. I said I wanted to pray for her and she agreed. So I prayed like this:

Father God I praise and thank you that you have promised to hear us when we pray. I praise you Jesus that your death and resurrection give us the right to come into the presence of the most high God and make our concerns known. I praise you for Isabella and thank you that she is one of yours. That her name is written in the Lamb's Book of Life and that her name is written on your hand. I praise you for your continuing care for Isabella. Today, I want to praise you Jesus for your promise that you came to bring life and life in all its fullness. I praise you that you are able to reach down and bring your miraculous healing power to Isabella and restore her to a full life, not one lived in a hospital room. I praise you that you are able to renew her body without a transplant. I praise you because I know you are able to restore Isabella to a state of health that is beyond anything she can even imagine. I admit it wasn't looking good. She hardly opened her eyes. It was difficult to find anything to talk about. I'd like to say what a great feeling of peace I had along with the knowledge that God had heard my prayer and was going to act. I'd like to, but I can't, as I didn't feel any of those things. But my faith doesn't depend on feelings. I knew that God had given me a desire to pray for Isabella, had provided the finance to make the trip possible and slotted it into my busy life. Why would he go to all the trouble if he wasn't prepared he heal her? I don't try to understand God's ways; they are much too complicated for me.

A couple of days later, I was on Facebook when I spotted that Isabella had tagged me in a post. She had uploaded photos of the chocolates along with quotes from the ludicrously extravagant descriptions. She seemed to be so much better. And she was. Another entry described a trip out to a local restaurant. The following week, she was well enough to leave hospital. Personally, I had been overjoyed to find that job vacancy and to be offered an interview. Although keen to get a new job and really keen to get that particular job, I know that God often has another agenda. I didn't get that job, but I did get the opportunity to pray with my friend.

When we insist on asking, aren't we insisting on our own terms? In Luke 9 57-62. The would be followers of Jesus wanted to dictate their own terms.

As they were walking along the road, a man said to him, 'I will follow you wherever you go.'
Jesus replied, 'Foxes have dens and birds have nests, but the Son of Man has nowhere to lay his head.'
He said to another man, 'Follow me.'
But he replied, 'Lord, first let me go and bury my father.'
Jesus said to him, 'Let the dead bury their own dead, but you go and proclaim the kingdom of God.'
Still another said, 'I will follow you, Lord; but first let me go back and say goodbye to my family.'
Jesus replied, 'No one who puts a hand to the plough and looks back is fit for service in the kingdom of God.'

Anyone using a plough who looks back to check the furrows are straight will then find while they are looking back, the furrows become wiggly. It's important that furrows are straight as this enables the farmer to see the crop and remove the weeds. In a straight furrow, the crop will grow in a straight line so anything not growing in the line is a weed. The only way to get straight furrows is for the ploughman to keep their eyes in front, looking forward. If we want to dictate the terms of our following Christ then we have already failed. True discipleship requires the abandonment of our own desires and that includes the desire to request certain solutions to our problems. While we are making demands of God we are making demi gods of ourselves. How much more powerful would our prayer lives be if we gave up any claim to be part of the solution and gave all the glory to God?   Dietrich Bonhoeffer called this 'costly grace'.

The church where we do Nightchurch is ancient. There's been a church on that site since 400 AD and the current building has been there since 800 AD. But the church is now in the middle of a pedestrianised zone in the centre of the city's shopping area. Few, if any, people live nearby. There's no natural congregation. A small number of people still worship there and although the church is well used during the week, regular Sunday worship had been reduced to once a month. The one thing the remaining worshippers wanted was a big enough congregation to enable the church to hold Sunday services every week. It just seemed impossible. But we need to remember that with God, all things are possible. Seeming impossible didn't stop us believing that God could do it. But even we were surprised by the speed it happened.

I went to a party at the house of an old friend who I hadn't seen for some time. She started telling me how the church she attended in a school had decided they wanted a more permanent home and had asked the bishop to find them one. I started to get goosebumps. I just knew what she was going to say. I found it really hard to just listen. I so wanted to interrupted her with "You're going to tell me your church has moved into the Nightchurch church aren't you". Because that was what had just been agreed. A whole church, of predominately young families became the new Sunday congregation at our Nightchurch church. An answer to a prayer that we could not even imagine could be answered. We didn't need to dream up the solution. All we needed was to trust God.

Praying without asking is about changing our attitudes. If we have a negative attitude or are always looking for what we can get out of life we limit how much God will bless us. If we have a positive attitude and assume that everything that happens to us is for good then we will look for the good in situations. Being positive and remembering what God has done for us keeps us expecting more. Try it.

Paul and Silas praised God in a difficult situation and the result was an earthquake. I can't guarantee an earthquake. Actually maybe I can.

Chapter 6
Not praying, but listening

It could be that you don't see yourself as a prayer. Perhaps it isn't your particular gift or talent. Perhaps you are more practical. I don't see prayer as something restricted to only certain people. We are all called into a relationship with God. The only way we can develop that relationship is by spending time with God. I often find that churches don't have difficulty in finding people to help out with the day to day stuff. People will put the chairs out or make tea after the service. But ask them to pray before the service, suddenly; few people think this is important. But God made us as human beings. Why do we insist on being human doings?
It could be that we are not convinced that God wants to hear from us. We are happy enough to ask God for stuff, often because we don't have an alternative. But do we think that God wants us to turn up just to hang out with him? That is exactly what God wants. In Genesis, God walked in the Garden of Eden in the evenings to meet with Adam & Eve. He's still seeking the same informal relationship with us.
I am very blessed in that my daughter and two of my grandsons live very close by. A couple of

afternoons a week I pop in to see them on my way home from work. The boys are usually pleased to see me. Sometimes they cheer when I arrive; sometimes they rush up to say 'Hello' and tell me their news. Other times they are absorbed in an activity and barely notice my arrival. Mostly, they hide and I have to wander round thinking aloud as to where they might be, while deliberately not seeing them or hearing the muffled giggles when I pass close by before finally bursting out of their hiding places. I can never predict exactly what reception I will receive. Sometimes they have something they are keen to tell me. Other times finding out what they've been up to can be like getting blood out of a stone even when I know there is something they could tell me. Equally, when I leave, they might say goodbye, I might get a desultory wave or they might ignore me. Occasionally, they will say I can't go home or demand to come home to play at my house.

I don't visit my grandsons out of a sense of duty. I don't sigh and think I have too much to do to spend an hour or so with them after work. There are always other things I could do with that time. It does mean dinner might be late. It does mean housework is left undone. But spending time with these boys is always a joy. It is one of the favourite parts of my week. I find time because they are important to me. Because I enjoy their company. One of the things I really like about our relationship is that they know when we get together that I will almost always give them my undivided attention. I don't spend time doing housework or anything else. Perhaps most importantly, they never ask me for anything other than my attention. There certainly isn't any cupboard love here. At my house, I have games and toys and of course, a stock of chocolate frogs, but I don't believe they visit just for these. What we do or say when we get together isn't important. Sometimes when I visit they are already busy, perhaps they have a friend round to play. Other times they are tired out. I don't need to measure the success of my visits. If they don't interact much with me I don't decide that I wasted my time visiting. What we talk about or do when we're together is not important.

What's important is that we spend time together. Even on the days that they largely ignore me, what matters is that I turned up. I know they will remember that Nanny came to see them often.

Even when they were very small and didn't interact with me much, they still noticed if I went away and didn't visit for a few days.

Shouldn't our relationship with God be like this? Surely we should think of God as someone whose company we enjoy rather than someone who can do stuff for us?

I don't believe that the words we pray are the most important part. What matters is taking time to seek the presence of God. We don't have to worry that something won't happen unless we badger God for it. We just need to turn up. We don't need to ask for anything. Actually, we don't need to say anything at all.

Prayer shouldn't just be about us talking. It's a two-way conversation so that means we should be listening too. Most of us know someone who talks a lot, someone who dominates the conversation and talks about themself or about topics that concern them or voices their opinions at length. Think about the conversations you have with that person, are they the most enjoyable ones you have? Probably not. Management Consultants tell us that the best way to appear interesting and to leave a good impression is to listen and not talk. Apparently, the people we consider most interesting are those who in fact, are interested, and interested in us. It's actually very difficult to have a close friendship with a person who never stops to listen. If a close relationship with God is our aim, then our conversations needs to be at least 50% listening.

1 Peter 5:7 Living Bible
Let him have all your worries and cares, for he is always thinking about you and watching everything that concerns you.

Let him have all your worries and cares. The keyword here is 'have'. Let him have all your cares and to do that, we need to let go of them and allow them to become his, not ours. If we come to prayer and we keep on and on at God, we aren't bringing our problems to God and leaving them there, we're bringing our problems to God but still hanging onto them. We need to do exactly what Peter said. We need to let God

have all our worries and cares.
When we've managed to stop asking God to do stuff, the next step is to relax and believe that God has our best interests in his heart. I'm actually asking you not to even want God to do stuff. To forget about your needs and wants. This is hard. I'm asking that your prayers become about God, rather than about you and your situation or even your concerns. It may require changing our attitudes. If we have a negative attitude or are always looking for what we can get out of life we limit how much God will bless us. If we have a positive attitude and assume that everything that happens to us is for good then we will look for the good in situations. We will know that there is good & look for it.

In Matthew 11 v 28-30, Jesus said this:

Come to me, all who are weary and heavy laden, and I will give you rest. Take my yoke upon you, and learn from me; for I am gentle and humble of heart, and you will find rest for your soul. For my yoke is easy and my burden is light.

If your problems are weighing you down, then put them down. Give them to God and leave them with him.
A yoke is a wooden beam normally used between a pair of oxen or other animals to enable them to pull together on a load when working in pairs. The bad news is that this means work. Jesus didn't say he would lift weight off the heavy laden, he said his yoke

would make it easier and he wouldn't add to the burden. As Dietrich Bonhoeffer put it, discipleship is about discipline. Where will the call to discipleship lead? What decisions will it involve? Only Jesus Christ knows where the path will lead. But we know that it will be a path full of mercy beyond measure. Discipleship is joy.

Inevitably, we when we are praying, we are likely to run out of things to say. So rather than fill the space with anything, fill it with nothing. Use silence. When we are with people we don't know well and the conversation flags, we call that silence 'awkward' and find it really uncomfortable. With people we know well, we don't have to keep talking, we can cope with silence. In the same way, we should be able to be silent with God. Silence in prayer is difficult. But silence in God's presence is amazing, though it does take practice. Silence is a really important part of prayer. Not just because it's very difficult to hear God speak if we don't shut up, but because being silent with people we know well is ok.

When we are silent, we do give God a space to talk to us. Maybe he'll say something, maybe he won't. But if we never stop talking even God finds it a challenge to get through to us. (The good news is that he will find a way, but let's not make it difficult for him).

Inevitably, when I stop talking and try listening, then the rest of my life comes crashing in. I want to meditate on God but the moment I stop and try to listen, my mind is filled with all the decisions I need to make and the issues I need to deal with. Stopping this happening is not easy or simple. It takes time. There are strategies that can be employed to deal with this. Personally, I mentally check any issues into a cloakroom. I don't give them any attention. I don't try and think up solutions now. I just tell myself that they will still be waiting for me later, but right now I need to be silent. I don't let them take over, but just park them for a few minutes. I keep doing this until they stay there. It takes time. But when we do stop and clear space for God to speak to us, then we're likely to find that he does have something to say to us. If we don't let God get a word in edge ways it may take longer for us to find out everything he wants to tell us.

There are times when perhaps we don't want to hear what God has to say. God gave me a message for member of my church. Her foster daughter was seriously ill. It was a simple message - he said, "Please stop talking and let me speak. I have something to tell you". I told her and she burst into tears. "I know what he wants to say and I don't want to hear it," she said. "He's going to tell me she's not going to live". She agreed she was refusing to listen, as she didn't think she could deal with what God might say. It's not a strategy I would recommend. I hoped she had the courage to listen. A few weeks later the girl did lose her fight for life but the foster mum coped with it really well. When God speaks to us it is never to make us miserable. He may discipline us but it will never make us feel depressed or hopeless.

Spending time with God grows our relationship with him. What may seem difficult at first will become easier with practice until it becomes automatic. Long before it became easy for me, I found that I so enjoyed seeking the presence of God; I would jump out of bed in the morning eager to start. It does all take time.

In 'Experiencing the depths of Jesus Christ' Jeanne Guyon suggests looking inside yourself to find God.

'The Lord is found only within our spirit, in the recesses of your being, in the Holy of Holies; this is where he dwells. The Lord once promised to come and make his home within you (John 14 v 23). He promised to there meet with those who worship Him and do His will. The Lord will meet you in your spirit It was St Augustine who once said that he had lost much time in his Christian experience by trying to find The Lord outwardly rather than by turning inwardly'.

Jeanne Guyon described a state of abandonment. Not that we are abandoned but one in which we voluntary leave our problems.

One in which we have dropped all our needs. Our physical needs, our spiritual needs, all of them are abandoned and in their place is the knowledge that God cares for us and already knows all our problems, our needs and even our desires.

Matt 6v32
Take no thought for tomorrow for your Heavenly Father knows that you have need of all these things.

Practice abandonment by continually losing your will in the will of God. It requires us to forget our past, to cease worrying about the future and to spend the present in God's presence. It requires us to be satisfied now, because we know are in the will of God. It means giving up our reactions to what happens to us and accepting that God will work everything together for good. Above all, it requires us to stop worrying.

Why do we seek the presence of God? Because he is our Father and we are his children. As Jeanne Guyon puts it

'Consider the servant. The servant takes good care of his master; but does it only to receive some reward. He is not worthy of any consideration whatsoever. So dear Christian, as you come to your Lord to pray, do not come for spiritual enjoyment. Do not even come to experience your Lord. Then what? Come just to please Him.'

When we seek God's presence in this way, when we pray without needing to ask, the difference between spiritual dryness and spiritual richness will disappear. For in both times we are seeking God, not because he speaks to us or because we feel his presence but we seek him only to worship him.

I wonder how many times God tried to talk to Paul? Striking someone blind on a desert road

doesn't seem likely to me to be where God would like to start. We can only guess, but I am sure God will have tried a few times to get through to Paul. I know a man who I would describe as an intellectual agnostic. He used to say that he thought God was unknowable by humans. He is very intelligent and a great thinker. His wife was a Christian, but he was very dismissive of her faith. One day, this man's wife announced she was leaving. He was devastated. She said he was selfish. "When we married" she said to me "I thought he was Mr. Right. I didn't know his first name was Always". She told me that she'd prayed consistently during their 19 year relationship that he would become a Christian. She was beginning to give up. One day, he was having a go about her faith and he said, "I just hate religion".
"So do I" she snapped back.
"But you go to church to be told what to believe". She'd laughed at him and said he didn't have a clue what church was about. She did feel bad about being sarcastic, but it was this exchange that marked the turning point. A few weeks later, he asked he a very simple question, "What is it that you believe?" She says that she'd stopped caring what he thought of her and was planning a new life without him. So she told him what she believes. Suddenly, this man started thinking about God and asked her if he could come to church with her and reluctantly, she agreed.
Less than four weeks later, he became a Christian. He told me that God said to him that he'd tried several times to get in touch. The man

had been diagnosed with an incurable illness; God said he'd tried then. Then the couple's first baby could have died during labour, but was saved by the man's wife going to hospital and telling them there was a problem with her baby & the hospital responding with an emergency C-section. God tried then, but again was ignored.

It was only when his wife said she was leaving that the man heard God speaking and became a Christian. And yes, his wife came back to him, because he became more understanding, less selfish and got more involved in her life.

Sometimes, we think we can hear what God is saying but are we always right? A young man I knew told me he believed that God was calling him into the ministry to be a pastor. So he stopped working and waited for God to tell him what to do next. But in the Bible, no one ever seems to have called from idleness into God's work. Peter was a fisherman. Mathew was a tax collector. Moses looked after his father in laws sheep. All I know is that more than 30 years later, the man is approaching retirement age and has never become a pastor.

A friend of mine visited a church in another part of the country. She felt God say to her that the vicar who was preaching that morning would become the Rector of our church. Not long afterwards, our Rector retired and a new man was appointed. It was not the man whose church she had visited. The effect on my friend was quite severe. She became depressed. She was sure that God had told her something but it hadn't turned out to be true. The new Rector wasn't here long before personal circumstances caused him to resign. The new Rector? Yep, the vicar my friend had met. It's important to listen to God carefully. Even when we think we must have misheard, we need to remember that we might not have misheard it all. Like my friend, we may only have added the word 'next' to what God said. God said that vicar would become our Rector. She added to what God said to make it 'the next Rector'.

God gave me a message for a member of my church, a woman I knew well. I didn't want to deliver it. She isn't the kind of person who would easily accept a message. I resisted for weeks until sitting in church one Sunday, I felt God physically poking me in the ribs and insisting I deliver the message. She came straight up to me after church and I gave her the message. It did not go down well. She was absolutely furious. Not at the message, but that it had come indirectly. "If God had a message for me" she said, "He would tell me himself". In theory, she was right. But sometimes we're just not listening. An important part of prayer is giving time to God to reply. If we carry on talking, how will we hear what God has to say? So quiet in prayer time is important. As an update on our relationship, we're now really good friends. And yes, she did eventually accept the message I delivered. But should we really be dictating to God how he should deliver a message? I think what she learnt that day was more than was contained in the message.

Chapter 7 How not to pray

Praying without asking also cuts out the need for those prayers that make us a tad uneasy - the ones where someone declares that we releasing the power of the Holy Spirit in our meeting. Do we actually have the authority to do that? I don't think so. Or someone tries to bind up the Enemy and crush all his works? Not convinced we can do that either. If we can, why hasn't it been done? I've heard a man call for angels to come down from heaven. I'm not sure why, as he didn't give a reason, only the request. I am sure that we can't make these kinds of demands on God. What was the point of praying like this? Let's not worry about what we can and can't ask for, let's just praise God.

Just as importantly, praying without asking puts a stop to prayers that should never be said, prayers against people or situations. I don't hear of them often but I wish I never heard of them at all. In his book 'Blessings and Curses' Derek Prince cites the case of a pastor whose daughter was engaged to a man from a different denomination. A Christian, but not one the pastor would have chosen for his daughter. He prayed against their relationship and eventually she broke off the engagement and married a non-Christian instead. I am sure that is not what the Pastor wanted, but he only prayed negatively and he got what he asked for - the ending of her relationship.

A friend of mine admitted to me that she had been praying for God to remove her minister from his post as in her opinion, he was fairly useless. She went on to tell me that she began to realise that having an ineffective minister meant that people in the church began to step up and take on roles that they hadn't before. If the minister had been better at his job, there wouldn't be a need for them to help out and she doubts they would have. But she watched as people took on a greater share of the ministry and she realised that their development had only happened because of the shortcomings of the minister. Because of his weakness, the church members have grown in strength. I've no doubt that the church has been built into a effective team that is not only is making up for the shortfall in their ministry of their leader, but in the future, when a new minister does take over, s/he will find a capable, hardworking and effective team already in place. God does actually know what he's doing and does work everything out for good.

After my divorce, I met a man I wanted to marry but he wasn't a Christian. A friend and I prayed and we both felt God saying it was ok, he would become a Christian. Just before our wedding, I received a phone call from a close member of my family. He was ringing to tell me not to go ahead with the wedding. The Bible is clear, he insisted, that Christians should not marry non-Christians. He refused to attend the wedding. Clearly, one of us had got it wrong. I wonder if he prayed against my marriage. I hope not, as my husband has become a Christian. If he had just thanked God that God is in control of my life, he would have saved himself a great deal of stress.

A friend of mine was appalled when her teenage daughter came home with a tattoo. It wasn't just that she had a tattoo but that she was under 18 and the law says that under 18s must not be tattooed. My friend wanted to pray against the tattooist's business but when she did so, God told her to stop and told her instead to bless the man and the business. Against her wishes she did so. Two weeks later, he died. How would she be feeling now if she had prayed against his business? Now she knows that the tattooist did not own the business, but was only managing it for the owners. After, his death, the owners found out their manger had gained a reputation as someone who is willing to flount the law and tattoo underage girls. They were appalled and resolved to take a more active interest in the running of their business in future. Now she knows that praying against the business just wasn't the right thing to do.

I wonder how much more of this is going on? How many people are praying negative prayers? Against people, against situations, even against people's ministries? Let's put a stop to it now.

Chapter 8 The power of praise

Psalm 22 v 3 NIV
But you are holy,   you who inhabit the praises of Israel.
God inhabits praise. That's why, when we praise, we often become aware of the presence of God. If we want to experience the presence of God more often, then praise is the key.
Isaiah had a vision of God, recorded in Isaiah chapter 6. We know he was in the temple so it seems likely he was worshipping God when his worship brought God down from heaven. When we praise we give glory to God and by doing so bring heaven down to earth. Heaven is full of God's praises. A new intercessor joined the prayer room at Nightchurch. I explained to her my belief that we should be praying & not asking. She said she was prepared to join in and we began praising God without asking for anything. During the evening, another volunteer joined us and immediately asked for a Bible. She began reading Isaiah 6 out loud.
NIV
In the year that King Uzziah died, I saw the Lord, high and exalted, seated on a throne; and the train of his robe filled the temple. Above him were seraphim, each with six wings: with two

wings they covered their faces, with two they covered their feet, and with two they were flying. And they were calling to one another:
'Holy, holy, holy is the Lord Almighty;
the whole earth is full of his glory.'
At the sound of their voices the doorposts and thresholds shook and the temple was filled with smoke.

"These seraphim" she said "These six winged angels that Isaiah saw, there's two by the door". I didn't see them myself but I wasn't surprised that two seraphim had come down from heaven to join in with our praises.

Do we have any idea of the power of praise? We know praise is important. Jesus said if people stopped praising the stones would cry out. We do know that praise reduces the power of the Enemy. He can't stand to be in the presence of God's praise. When we praise we give glory to God. When I have a problem, instead of going on and on at God about it, I praise him for the times he has solved problems for me in the past. By doing this, I am declaring two things, one that God is all powerful and does answer prayers and two, that I am putting my faith in God.

When we praise we stop worrying about our problems. It isn't possible to praise & worry about our problems any more than it is possible to sneeze with our eyes open. Once we start praising God we stop worrying about our problems. The Enemy uses our problems to stop us praising. How happy he must be with prayer meeting after prayer meeting where the focus remains firmly on our problems instead of on God. When we endlessly whinge about problems and demand solutions. If we want to see God move in power, we need to acknowledge our faith in his power. Praise is the voice of faith. If we really believe God has heard our prayers, we will start praising Him for the answer, even before we see it. When you're tempted to feel down and discouraged, remember the power of praise and look to God.

What happens when we praise?

Psalm 9 v 3 Living Bible
My enemies will fall back and perish in your presence.

How do our enemies get into the presence of God? It can only be that praise brings God down to us. When we praise and worship God, we become more aware of his presence. When Paul & Silas praised while chained up in prison an earthquake freed them. But look what else happened:

Acts 16 v 29-31 The Message

The jailer got a torch and ran inside. Badly shaken, he collapsed in front of Paul and Silas.

He led them out of the jail and asked, "Sirs, what do I have to do to be saved, to really live?"

Praise didn't just release Paul and Silas from their prison chains; it also led to the jailer being saved. When we praise God, we make it more likely that he will act.

We do know that praise reduces the power of the Enemy. He can't stand to be in the presence of God's praise. Consider Job. He had much to praise God for but he continued praising God even when it was taken away.

Job 1 1-3, 8-11 The Message.

Job was a man who lived in Uz. He was honest inside and out, a man of his word, who was totally devoted to God and hated evil with a passion. He had seven sons and three daughters. He was also very wealthy—seven thousand head of sheep, three thousand camels, five hundred teams of oxen, five hundred donkeys, and a huge staff of servants—the most influential man in all the East.

God said to Satan, "Have you noticed my friend Job? There's no one quite like him—honest and true to his word, totally devoted to God and hating evil."

Satan retorted, "So do you think Job does all that out of the sheer goodness of his heart? Why, no one ever had it so good! You pamper him like a pet, make sure nothing bad ever happens to him or his family or his possessions, bless everything he does—he can't lose!

"But what do you think would happen if you reached down and took away everything that is his? He'd curse you right to your face, that's what."

But despite the loss of all his children and of all his wealth, Job did not blame God.

Job 1 v 21-22 The Message

Naked I came from my mother's womb, naked I'll return to the womb of the earth. God gives, God takes. God's name be ever blessed. Not once through all this did Job sin; not once did he blame God.

The source of Job's praise was the almighty nature of God. He didn't praise God because God had blessed him; God blessed him because Job was thankful. Losing all his possessions and even his children did not stop Job from praising God because it didn't change who God is. Are we on cupboard love? We'll thank God if we think there is something in it for us? I hope not.
If we praise God despite our situation is it more powerful? I suggest it is. Praising God for good situations is so easy. Praising God anyway is a challenge but if we can do it, it seems the value is greater. Consider the story of the widow's mite. Jesus described her contribution to be worth more than the generous contributions of the rich because they gave out of their plenty & she gave all she had. Praising God when we feel we have little to thank God for has two impacts. One, we search & find something to be thankful for ('I may have lost my job but I'm healthy') and two; the value to God is greater. Praising in the bad times shows that ours isn't just cupboard love. We don't just praise God because of what

we get but because of who he is.
We don't fully understand the power of words but there is some evidence that to quote secular research 'people make their own luck'. Job said '

The worst of my fears has come true, what I've dreaded most has happened. Job 3 v 25 The Message

Consider this tale. A friend of mine asked me to sign her passport application. She told me she really feared that her new passport would get lost in the post. To avoid this she arranged to take the application form into the passport office personally and paid extra for the courier delivery of her new passport, which guaranteed delivery of the new passport within eight days. At exactly the same time, I was renewing three of our passports. I put the forms in the post and eight days later, our three new passports arrived. My friend's did not. The Passport Office assured her that the courier company had confirmed it had been delivered. But it had not. The one thing she feared had happened. Her passport was lost. I prayed about it and then suggested she visit the local postal sorting office. Sure enough, there was her passport. The courier had delivered it to the wrong street. The occupant, assuming the postman had delivered it, popped it into the postbox. The sorting office refused to deliver it as no postage had been paid on it. The thing she feared came upon her. If negative words can have a negative impact on our lives, how much more powerful are words of praise?

Just weeks after I started praying without asking, we were watching a DVD one Saturday night when our electricity went off at 10.30pm. We checked the fuse box but didn't find anything wrong. I looked at the other houses in the street but most were in darkness which didn't help much. Maybe they were already in bed or still out. The lampposts were still lit. We decided to go to bed and hope it was fixed in the morning. It wasn't. After church, we rang Dave, an electrician friend who told us there was virtually no incoming current to our meter so we reported the fault. Very quickly, an assessor arrived followed a couple of hours later by a repair team who proceeded to dig up the pavement in order to find the fault. The hours wore on. This was February. We were without electricity, central heating, hot water and lighting. All we had was a gas hob and a wood burning stove. So why do I remember that day as being great fun? My daughter came round with her two small boys. They were mesmerised by the mini digger the workmen were using and stood on the sofa looking out of the window. Intermittently saying

"Look Nanny, digger". We kept a kettle on the wood burning stove and that kept us well supplied with tea. We heated up left over chilli, which was enough to feed everyone. The workmen were now digging up a second section of pavement. I joked "I'll know God loves me if they start digging up the sunken part of our drive". I was joking. I know God loves me anyway. But moments later, the workman abandoned their second hole and began digging hole number three - in the sunken part of the drive. We were without electricity for 22 hours. We couldn't watch the tv, use the internet or even listen to the radio. It was a dull February day but as the light began to fade, Dave decided the 30 amps or so which were still coming into the meter were enough to run the lights. We had lights, we were warm, had hot food, hot drinks and good company. Eventually, at about 8.30pm, our power was restored. We checked the freezer and found most of the food still perfectly frozen. All except the ice cream, which was going a bit soft so we were obliged to eat it. Within a couple of days, the restoration team came out, filled both holes in the pavement and re-laid our drive, making it much better than before. It wasn't a brilliant situation, being without electricity for 22 hours in February, but we had fun and ended up with a beautifully re-laid drive. For free. I am sure that praising made all the difference. None of us sat and fretted over when the electricity would be restored. Not even the teenagers complained about the lack of internet or the inability to charge their phones – a miracle surely? Did we need to fret? No. Was there anything at all to worry about? No. God had it all under control.

The apostle Paul didn't always have a trouble free existence as he explained to the church at Corinth:

2 Corinthians 11 v 23-27 The Message
I've worked much harder, been jailed more often, beaten up more times than I can count, and at

death's door time after time. I've been flogged five times with the Jews' thirty-nine lashes, beaten by Roman rods three times, pummelled with rocks once. I've been shipwrecked three times, and immersed in the open sea for a night and a day. In hard traveling year in and year out, I've had to ford rivers, fend off robbers, struggle with friends, struggle with foes. I've

been at risk in the city, at risk in the country, endangered by desert sun and sea storm, and betrayed by those I thought were my brothers. I've known drudgery and hard labor, many a long and lonely night without sleep, many a missed meal, blasted by the cold, naked to the weather.

But still Paul insists we should praise in all circumstances. If he could, why can't we?
Soon after I stopped asking and started praising I had an uncomfortable experience. I was out walking and praising as usual early one morning, as I turned a corner with my dog, I became aware of someone shouting. I looked up and saw a woman walking a dog. She was shouting abuse apparently at me. I couldn't make out much of what she was saying partly because she was so angry and partly because what she was saying was so liberally sprinkled with the f word. I think she was upset that I had walked around the corner and was now walking on the same pavement as her. My dog is very friendly and quite gentle so I wouldn't cross the road to avoid a dog unless the other dog was showing aggression but in any case, I'd never seen her or

her dog as I turned the corner. I'd been looking at my dog. I am still puzzled by her aggression. It seemed quite out of proportion. This was not destined to be an isolated incident. Sometimes I would see her marching along at top speed with her head held high. Unlike almost all the other dog walkers, I never saw her stop and chat with the other walkers. Mostly, she would totally ignore me but occasionally, she would hurl more vitriolic foul-mouthed abuse at me as she walked her dog along the other side of the road. There didn't seem to be any rhyme or reason to her shouting. It didn't seem to matter if she was walking on the same side of the road as us or if she'd always been on the other side. Sometimes she would shout and sometimes she would ignore me. Thankfully, I only saw her occasionally. I put it down to my praise walking having an impact in the spirit world - another reason to praise. But it was still disconcerting to be shouted at. One summer, we took in another rescue dog, underweight and found in the street. No one even knew her name or how old she was. She was probably about 8-10 months old. We called her Cassie and she joined me on my morning praise walks. Then one day, we saw the shouty woman. This time, she didn't shout as we walked by, but stood on the other side of the road and hurled personal abuse at me and at Cassie. And this time, unlike all the others, I heard exactly what she said. It was nasty, untrue, a pack of lies. I ignored her and carried on walking. But it still upset me.

That lunchtime, I popped to the supermarket

near where I work. A middle-aged woman came up to me from behind. She touched me on the back and asked, "Do you have dogs?" It seemed an odd question. Surely most dog owners have just the one, but she said "dogs", plural. I admitted I have two. She asked me about them interspersing her questions with information and anecdotes about her own dogs. It was a really surreal conversation. I told her about Cassie, how we'd taken her in. She touched my arm and said, "You're doing everything right for that dog". Then she said, "You are the right person to be caring for that dog". Astonishingly, she went on to refute everything shouty woman had said to me that morning. I never mentioned my experience that morning to her but it seemed to me that she just knew. So I just stood there in the supermarket and listened as she unsaid all the nasty, negative lies that the shouty woman had hurled at me that morning. I don't know who she was but I became more and more certain that she had been sent by God to counteract those lies. It was an amazing experience. I heard the opposites of the insults I'd heard that morning. Now, when I think of that day, I don't think of shouty woman's lies, I think of the lovely woman in the supermarket. The damage shouty woman tried to inflict was completely removed and replaced with a bizarre but hugely positive experience. I relayed the story to a friend of mine who advised me to rebuke shouty woman if she tried to shout at me again and this resolved to do Not long afterwards, I was on the left side of a road, approaching a T junction, intending to turn left along the main road when I noticed shouty woman approaching the same junction but from the right, going straight along the main road in the same direction as me. We were on a collision course. I was ready to rebuke her if she started to shout at me. To my amazement, she bowed her head, spoke quietly to her dog and waited at the kerb, allowing me to go first. Then she crossed the main road, walked along the other side of the road at her usual top speed until she had overtaken me, crossed back to my side of the road quite a way in front of me and continued her walk. All the time, her head was bowed, not held high as it normally was. And she was silent. In fact, I've seen her since and each time, her head has been bowed and she remains silent. She has never shouted at me again. I am sure she never will again. Recently, my dog was doing his business close to the dog bin when she came along. We couldn't move away. She needed to get to the bin. I looked straight at her and said 'Good morning', she did not respond, but unlike all the other times, she carried on walking along the same side of the road as me. Praise is powerful. Although praise triggered the verbal attack on me, equally, I am sure that because I was praising, God refused to allow me to be hurt by the attack. I can't find anything in the Bible to say that those who praise will have an easy life or be prevented from being attacked by the enemy; God certainly protected me from being damaged. This is no prosperity gospel. It won't make you richer, give you a more comfortable lifestyle or immure you from troubles. Praise is not a protection from harm, ensuring that bad things will no longer happen or that life will become easier, more comfortable, more secure. On the contrary, praising God will attract the attention of the enemy

In fact, like me you may get verbal abuse in the street from those who your praises make uncomfortable. The apostle Paul praised in all circumstances and it didn't give him a nice cosy life. Far from it. It's thought that Paul was executed. He describes himself as about to be poured out like a drink offering. Praising in all circumstances will not bring financial security or a problem free life. What it will bring is a closer walk with God. It brings me more opportunities to talk about my faith and more opportunities to see God at work in the lives of those around me.

Chapter 9 Confession

Mark 11 v 25 The Message

If you have anything against someone, forgive—only then will your heavenly Father be inclined to also wipe your slate clean of sins."

1 John 1:8 NIV
If we claim to be without sin, we deceive ourselves and the truth is not in us.

Isaiah 64 v 6 The Living Bible
We are all infected and impure with sin. When we put on our prized robes of righteousness, we find they are but filthy rags.

Confession is a really big part of prayer. We need to confess our sins and to do that we actually need to be aware of what we're doing that is wrong. To do this we need to examine our behaviour, our words and our attitudes and admit to God when we get it wrong. The Bible clearly warns us that if we don't forgive other people, God won't forgive us and our prayers won't be heard.
It's easy to kid ourselves that our spirituality will cover up our sin. That somehow being close to

God means we don't sin. Hopefully, it means we sin less, but unfortunately, less doesn't count. Sin is sin. Isaiah, no slouch when it came to being spiritual, describes his righteousness as being like dressed in filthy rags. What he actually said is even worse than that. The Orthodox Jewish Bible uses the phrase 'beged iddim' and it is correctly translated in the Common English Bible. Most other translations have a sanitised version. Look it up if you really want to know how God views our sin.

James 5:14-16
Is anyone among you ill? Let them call the elders of the church to pray over them and anoint them with oil in the name of the Lord.
And the prayer offered in faith will make the sick person well; the Lord will raise them up. If they have sinned, they will be forgiven.
Therefore confess your sins to each other and pray for each other so that you may be healed. The prayer of a righteous person is powerful and effective.

The willingness to admit we need forgiveness is key to receiving God's blessing in our lives. It can be tempting for those who have been Christians for a long time to be lured into believing that we don't need forgiveness, we're just not that bad. We secretly believe that we're better than those who have never repented and excuse our shortcomings because we are sure God overlooks them. It's a position that risks rendering us powerless. Not only are we sinning, but we don't even realise it.

Luke 18:10-14
'Two men went up to the temple to pray, one a Pharisee and the other a tax collector.
The Pharisee stood by himself and prayed: "God, I thank you that I am not like other people – robbers, evildoers, adulterers – or even like this tax collector.
I fast twice a week and give a tenth of all I get."
'But the tax collector stood at a distance. He would not even look up to heaven, but beat his breast and said, "God, have mercy on me, a sinner."
'I tell you that this man, rather than the other, went home justified before God. For all those who exalt themselves will be humbled, and those who humble themselves will be exalted.'

God detests pride. Spiritual pride is just as detestable as any other kind. How many Christians secretly feel pride? Consider themselves better than the unsaved? Too many I suspect. Think you don't sin? Think again.
Harold Camping, was an American pastor who announced the date of second coming as 21st May 2011. When it was pointed out to him that the Bible says no one knows the day or the time Camping said that didn't apply to him as God had told him and him only. That was pride.

Matthew 24 36 The Message
"But the exact day and hour? No one knows that, not even heaven's angels, not even the Son.

Only the Father knows.

The angels don't know, even Jesus himself doesn't know but Harold Camping believed that God had told him. Camping believed he was extra special. So special that God would go against what was written in the Bible. That doesn't explain why he thought it was a good idea to announce it to the rest of the world. If God had actually told Harold Camping the date of the Second Coming then the statement in Matthew would not be true. If that is not true, then isn't the whole of the Bible undermined? If Matthew 24 isn't true, is the rest true? Harold Camping hadn't thought this through. His announcement actually undermined the faith he had believed in for so long.
Harold Camping was wrong. He was an extreme case, but how many of us are tempted to think like this? We are children of God. We are adopted in his family. But that does not mean we can sin and God won't notice. We often think that our weak points are where sin is most likely to gain entrance. But like Harold Camping, our strong points can be where we are tempted into sin too. With a double danger that we're not even considering that sin could creep in there. If we are talented singers, musicians or speakers then we can sin by believing in our own importance. It is so easy to slip into believing that God's work is happening because of us. That our ministry led to people becoming saved or healed or blessed. In doing so we make gods of ourselves. Sometimes there is a fine line

between acknowledging our talents and abilities and becoming arrogant. False humility is nauseating, but arrogance is sin.

In the case of Harold Camping, I don't believe his mistaken belief came about because of weakness, but of strength. Presumably God had spoken to him in the past and he was tempted to believe that this time he had heard something exclusive.

The story of Abraham is very well known. How Abraham and his wife Sarai were called by God to leave Ur of the Chaldees, a city in Mesopotamia that was so advanced it even had flushing toilets, and journey to the promised land – Canaan. Except there's a really important bit that usually gets missed out. It's this; find it in the end of the chapter before God calls Abraham.

Genesis 11 v 31 NIV
Terah took his son Abram, his grandson Lot (Haran's son), and Sarai his daughter in law (his son Abram's wife) and set out with them from Ur of the Chaldees for the land of Cannaan. But when they got as far as Haran, they settled there.
Terah lived 205 years. He died in Haran.

It sounds to me, like God called Terah to travel to the promised land. It clearly says that Terah left Ur to journey to Canaan, but he didn't get there. He got as far as Haran and stayed there. It wasn't until after Terah died, that God gave

Terah's call to Abraham. God is very gracious like that. It didn't happen in Terah's lifetime, but if we don't do what God is calling us to do, he will give our calling to someone else. No one is indispensable.

A Christian once said to me that she couldn't imagine finding something to ask forgiveness for everyday. She isn't unusual, I suspect that most people consider themselves to be not that bad. If we desire a closer walk with God then we need an awareness of the sin in our lives and not just the obvious stuff. My city recently held a Gay Pride festival. Some Christians demonstrated on the street and gave out leaflets containing warnings regarding 'the seven deadly sins'. I was intrigued. Having been brought up nonconformist, I don't know what these are and after reading their leaflet, I wasn't convinced they had the right seven. I searched online and found a different seven deadly sins to those in the leaflet. Theirs included homosexuality and adultery as two of the seven, whereas online, lust seemed to cover both and the online version had sloth, which was missing from the leaflet. I am not convinced that the two are so easily interchangeable but the leaflet got me thinking. How often do we grade sin? We label certain sins as worse than others and as long as we avoid these, convince ourselves that we are better than others. That somehow only committing less serious sins means we are closer to God than other people. The Bible is clear that there are no grades of sin. Sin is sin. I wonder if those who handed out those leaflets consider that they themselves sin and need to confess? Obviously, they aren't committing these 'deadly' sins. But the Bible is clear, all sin is deadly. The Bible lumps in envy, gossiping and boasting in with murder and sexual sin. For me, just as importantly, the Bible makes it clear that we are to love people. Giving out leaflets telling people they are bound for hell – how does that show God's love to people?

Revelation 21:8 New International Version - UK
But the cowardly, the unbelieving, the vile, the murderers, the sexually immoral, those who practice magic arts, the idolaters and all liars – they will be consigned to the fiery lake of burning sulphur. This is the second death.'

Who amongst us doesn't get even a little bit envious or is tempted to gossip, or do a bit of lying? There's a Facebook post that does the rounds. It says:
'share this post if there is someone alive today because you can't afford a hitman'.
Actually, wishing someone dead is no different to murder. The good news is that we just need to ask for forgiveness and God will forgive us. We don't need to carry round guilt nor are we destined to repeat our past behaviour. God will give us a new start. All we need to do is to accept it.

Hebrews 12 *v1-3* The Message
Do you see what this means—all these pioneers

who blazed the way, all these veterans cheering us on? It means we'd better get on with it. Strip down, start running—and never quit! No extra spiritual fat, no parasitic sins. Keep your eyes on Jesus, who both began and finished this race we're in. Study how he did it. Because he never lost sight of where he was headed—that exhilarating finish in and with God—he could put up with anything along the way: Cross, shame, whatever. And now he's there, in the place of honour, right alongside God. When you find yourselves flagging in your faith, go over that story again, item by item, that long litany of hostility he plowed through. That will shoot adrenaline into your souls!

The Bible is clear, sin holds us back in our spiritual life. I recommend confessing sins to other Christians. Confession brings freedom. It also helps us not to slip back as we know someone else knows what we've done. They're unlikely to be watching us and expecting us to slip back again, but knowing someone else knows can help to strengthen our resolve. It also makes us more vulnerable. When I confess something, I run the risk that the person could remind me of it or even worse tell someone else. It creates a link between us. The reality is that if a person gossiped about my confession, it would damage them much more that it damaged me. People wouldn't remember what they said about me. All that would be remembered is that this was a person who gossips private information. God wants us to be linked. He wants us to be a family. I would not confess something to someone I didn't know well.

Matthew 5 v23-24 The Message
"This is how I want you to conduct yourself in these matters. If you enter your place of worship and, about to make an offering, you suddenly remember a grudge a friend has against you, abandon your offering, leave immediately, go to this friend and make things right. Then and only then, come back and work things out with God.

If someone has something against you. Not if you have something against someone or you have done something to upset someone. If someone has something against you. Forgiving people who have upset us is usually a challenge for us. Too often, we prefer to hang on to the hurt we feel. We've been hurt and need something to show for it. Something to complain about. Forgiving means letting go of that hurt. It means accepting that we are not the centre of the universe. That there is something more important than justifying how hurt we feel. Forgiveness is much more important. I was in a study group once and we were talking about forgiveness. One of the women in my group declared that she could never forgive her ex-husband. She didn't even want to and wasn't going to try. As has happened so often before, I spoke first and thought after. I didn't know this women but I pointed out to her that forgiveness was non negotiable. If she wanted God to forgive her, she was obliged to forgive her ex. I went home and felt really bad. Not about what I'd said, but the way I said it. It wasn't said with love and I had no idea what she had suffered or why she felt she couldn't forgive him. I really could have been much kinder. I felt bad about it all week. I resolved to apologise for the way I'd spoken to her. I expected her to avoid me at the next study group but instead she came rushing up to me. I steeled myself for her anger but instead she thanked me profusely. She insisted I had been completely right. She admitted she had been holding onto the hurt but my direct approach had made her realise that she had to let it go. She said she'd prayed that night for help to forgive her ex and found it was going to be possible. Then she added that she had never known that forgiving felt so amazing. And I'd spent a whole week feeling guilty!

There are times when we want to forgive but we have genuinely been hurt and letting go of that hurt is just too difficult. Since helping to run an Alpha course for mums, I continued to run a Bible study group for these mums along with a good friend of mine. I'll call her Nina. Two of the mums told me that Nina had decided to start a new style of Bible study group and suggested I go along too. Nina told me I would not be welcome as her group was only for spiritual people and in her opinion, I didn't qualify and never would. I was completely devastated. If my friend that I'd worked alongside for years did not consider me to be spiritual, where had I gone wrong? I don't think I have ever felt more hurt. I just sat at home crying. Sunday was going to be a problem. I knew I couldn't worship God in the same church as the person who had hurt me so much. Another friend suggested I go to her church so I did. After the service I was having a cup of tea, when a woman came up to me. "You've been stabbed with a thorn of rejection" she announced. "And God himself is going to remove it". It was all very dramatic but I knew she was right about the first bit. I could only hope she was right about the second.

Back at home; I knew I was facing a big problem. Forgiving Nina was nonnegotiable. I had to do it. Except I couldn't. Every time I thought about her, I remembered what she said and I felt a pain in my ribs. It wasn't that I didn't want to forgive her, I just didn't know how. I went to see our Rector. He put the two of us together, which enabled Nina to repeat her hurtful statement. I looked at the Rector and can still remember his eyes widening until they looked like saucers. I got the impression he didn't agree with her. Or maybe he thought some things are better left unsaid. He asked us both to imagine how it would feel to forgive the other person. Nice try, but I could not even imagine what forgiveness would feel like. I was much too hurt.

So everyday, I told God that I wanted to forgive Nina but didn't know how. Everyday for three months. During those months, it didn't get any easier. The pain didn't lessen. Several of my friends had gone off to join Nina's new Bible study group so I'd lost the enjoyment of meeting up with them every week. I'd managed to go back to my church but I couldn't see an end to my pain. Then one Sunday morning, I was sitting in church in the post communion quiet bit, when I felt God say this to me:

"When Nina said those things to you she didn't hurt you. She hurt me. She chose to refuse to see me when she looked at you. That was her choice. It is not your fault. That hurt is not yours to carry, it's mine"

At that point, I felt a hand physically reach under my ribs and pull something out. I was completely stunned. The pain had gone. As the service ended, I stood up and saw Nina. The pain did not return. I no longer felt hurt. God had removed my thorn of rejection exactly as the woman at my friend's church had prophesied. I knew I had forgiven Nina totally and completely.

After church, I went home and just sat on the settee. Too stunned to take in what had just happened. I hadn't been home long when my phone rang. It was the friend who had originally invited me to join Nina's group, a really close friend. She asked if I was ok. I assured her I was fine. "Well you don't seem fine". She insisted. "I tried I talk to you over coffee after church and you're just not with it. I don't think you heard a word I said. Are you going down with flu?" So I told her what had just happened and she agreed she'd look like I looked if that had just happened to her. The question is, which would I prefer? To go through the rejection experience or not? I am in no doubt that the suffering was well worth it to receive such an amazing experience of the love of God.

In chapter 7, I talked about prayers that should not be prayed. Prayers against people and against situations. If you have prayed these kinds of prayers, however well meaning, then you need to ask God's forgiveness. Praying without asking means we don't tell God what solution we want. While sometimes this is hard, at all times, it's just a very good idea. God can see the bigger picture.

Rather than pray against people we need to bless them. We need to remember that they, like us, are made in the image of God. They too are potentially his children. It is not our place to sit in judgment on people. When we wish bad things to happen to people we are acting like we are God. When we bless people, we avoid this altogether.

The young daughter of a friend of mine had a baby who was born without a functioning digestive system. Baby was taken immediately to a specialist hospital where they tried to repair her. At four months old, she had never left hospital, nor had her mum who stayed in the hospital with her baby. Baby was unable to digest food, so was fed intravenously. About 4am one morning, God woke me up and told me to repent of not caring enough for the baby to pray for her regularly. God told me that the baby although born to a young mum and whose dad went to prison went she was just three weeks old, was as precious to him as any IVF baby. So I began to repent.

As I dropped my children off at school, my friend, the baby's granny, was waiting for me. "Baby is

failing to thrive," she told me. "She's losing weight". At 4 months old, Baby weighed just 7lbs. The hospital said they would try and operate one more time but it could be that they had reached the end of what they could do. I explained to my friend what God had told me and promised to continue to repent and to pray for her granddaughter. She was a bit surprised.
"I can't believe you're admitting this to me" she said. I couldn't believe it either.
That lunchtime, God said something else to me. He said it wasn't just me who had failed to care about the fate of the baby; he said my friend's church didn't care either as he rarely heard her prayed for. There was one thing I wanted - the opportunity to apologise to the baby in person.
Back at school to collect my children, my friend had another problem. She needed to see her granddaughter the following day, for perhaps the last time, but she doesn't drive, the hospital was some distance away and the friend who had been taking her regularly was not available. So I was given the opportunity I wanted to apologise in person. So I went and held the baby and
apologised to her. The following day she had her final operation. The hospital told her Mum that they couldn't find anything wrong so they attached her whole system together and said to start her on 30mls of milk. That was mid October. Baby began to thrive so well the hospital said she might even be well enough to go home by Christmas. She went home in November.
She is now a lively, perfectly healthy child who is

able to eat normally and has no residual effects from her very rocky start. Confession is powerful. Don't neglect it.

Chapter 10 Taking it further

Still praising when things go wrong.

1 Thessalonians 5:16 NIV
Be cheerful no matter what; pray all the time; thank God no matter what happens. This is the way God wants you who belong to Christ Jesus to live.

Eph 5 v 20 NIV
Always giving thanks to God the Father for everything, in the name of Jesus Christ.

Hold on a minute, be cheerful no matter what, give thanks for everything? Not just the good bits? Everything? The Amplified version makes Ephesians 5 v 20 even clearer:

At all times and for everything, giving thanks in the name of our Lord Jesus Christ to God the Father.

I wish I could tell you that spending time with God will result in the ending of all your problems but it won't. I began to spend half an hour a day in prayer while my non-Christian husband was at work. When he changed his job, he found it very odd that I wanted to get up at 6.30am. He refused to allow me to put the central heating on that early as on one else was up. He really did not understand why I wanted to get up so early. So on cold winter mornings, I would wrap myself up in a blanket. I didn't stop praying. There can be a worrying tendency among Christians to treat God like some sort of slot machine. Put a little bit in and you'll get lots out. The Prosperity Gospel has seduced many people because we want it to be true. An easy life is attractive. To get lots for little effort is tempting. One of my favorite lines from a tv show is from the Blackadder III episode Nob and Nobility. It goes like this: Blackadder approaches le Comte de Frou Frou a French aristocrat who has recently escaped Revolutionary France and has taken refuge in Mrs Miggins' pie shop.

"How would you like to earn lots of money?" Blackadder asks Frou Frou.

I'd like other people to earn money and give it all to me just like in the good old days," replies Frou Frou.

But prayer can't be like that. Prayer needs to be for the glory of God, not because praying lots makes our lives better. If we pray to make our lives easier, then prayer is about us and not about God.

Hebrews 13:15 NIV
Through Jesus, therefore, let us continually offer to God a sacrifice of praise – the fruit of lips that openly profess his name.

A sacrifice of praise. The clue is in the word sacrifice. If it were easy it would be a joy. But it isn't. It's a sacrifice. We shouldn't just praise when our lives are going well and we feel like praising God. We should praise him at all times. I won't pretend that this isn't a challenge.

The thing is, praise shouldn't be about us. It must be about God. God doesn't change just because things are not how we wish. On days when the sky pours with rain we know the sun is still shining in the sky, even though we can't actually see the sun, we can see it's light. Our not being able to see the sun doesn't change the fact that the sun is shining, just as it does when there are no clouds in the way. Our praises should not depend on how we feel; they must depend on the unchanging nature of God. If we don't want to be fair weather Christians, only praising God when everything is going our way, then we need to continue to praise in difficult circumstances. Praise isn't about how we feel; we praise God because he is great and that does not change. If we only praise when things are going well, we risk becoming religious junkies, always craving the next fix of seeing God do something for us or being aware of his presence. It's not easy to be thankful when our troubles seem to pile higher than our blessings, when we manage it, I believe our praise becomes more valuable. As a weapon it becomes more effective. As a sword it becomes sharper. It's easy enough to praise God when things are going well but in the same way that Jesus told us to love our enemies and bless

those who hate us. Loving our friends is easy; the challenge is to love our enemies. It's what marks us out as different. If we praise God because of our blessings or even because worship gives us a nice warm feeling, our focus is on ourselves.
Where is the sacrifice? When we praise despite our problems, then our focus is on God.

Look at Isaiah 61:2-3 NIV

To proclaim the year of the Lord's favour and the day of vengeance of our God to comfort all who mourn, and provide for those who grieve in Zion –to bestow on them a crown of beauty instead of ashes, the oil of joy instead of mourning, and a garment of praise instead of a spirit of despair. They will be called oaks of righteousness a planting of the Lord for the display of his splendour.

A garment of praise for those who mourn. It doesn't say he will take away the cause of their mourning. It does say that those who wear this 'garment of praise' will become a 'display of his splendour'.

The Old Testament prophet Habakkuk knew about praising God in difficult circumstances: Habbakuk Chapter 3 v 17-18 NIV

Though the fig tree does not bud and there are no grapes on the vines, though the olive crop fails and the fields produce no food, though

there are no sheep in the pen and no cattle in the stalls, yet I will rejoice in the LORD, I will be joyful in God my Saviour.

Habakkuk is describing a really serious situation. It's not just the lack of food, without sheep; there is no wool for clothes, without cattle, no leather. But even worse, this isn't a short term problem, it's a long term desolation - no grapes on the vine means not only will there not be any grapes this year, it also means there won't be any wine or raisins throughout the next year. Figs take 2 years to grow so no buds this year doesn't just mean no fresh figs this year it means no fresh figs next year either, no dried figs for the next year or the year after. Habakkuk was talking about a situation that threatens our very survival. A situation that has no end in sight.
This isn't easy. But I'm saying we should praise God, not just in difficult circumstances but when we cannot see an end to our problems. Can we do that?

On the road to Emmaus, Jesus walked along beside two men. They didn't recognise him. Were they too wrapped up in how everything appeared to have gone wrong that they failed to see the bigger picture? They failed to see that Jesus was walking along beside them. How often is that us? How often do we focus on our problems and fail to recognise that Jesus is walking with us? Is it that we don't expect to see him? And because we aren't expecting to see him, we don't? How different it would be if we expected to see him, expected him to act in our present situation?

If we can get to the point where we can praise God despite things going wrong then the next step is to praise God *because* things have gone wrong. The good news is that it's a much smaller step! It does require complete abandonment into the knowledge that God is in control. It does require us to focus completely on God. But there is a huge amount of stress free, relaxed living available to those who take the step. I've done my share of ranting at God and struggling to understand how he could possibly allow some things to happen to me. But I am now beginning to understand what Paul meant when he said:

And we know that in all things God works for the good of those who love him.
Romans 8 v 28 NIV

All things work together for good. Not just the nice bits. The good, the not so good and the downright nasty. All things. Sometimes, it might not be for our good. It might be for someone else's. A friend of mine had a couple of miscarriages. Then, at 18 weeks pregnant found her baby could not be born alive. Without kidneys or lungs, he was unlikely to go to term. She was devastated and I admit it was hard for me with four healthy children to really understand how she felt. I could imagine, but I didn't know. Later on, when I was 12 weeks pregnant with baby number five, I was worried there was a problem. The hospital were very nice & got out a portable scanner. I know what a 12-week-old baby looks like and it was clear to me, that wasn't a 12-week-old baby on the screen, just a motionless sphere. No heartbeat. Baby had died 5 weeks before. There was only one person I wanted to see - my friend with the lost babies. I sat in her house, still carrying a dead baby. I don't remember her saying anything because there is nothing that can be said in a situation like this. But I knew she understood exactly how I felt and that gave me comfort. The good that came out of her lost babies is that she understands perfectly and can comfort those who suffer the same tragedy. When we suffer inexplicable tragedies we can reach out to those who are in pain and say 'I know how you feel'. And we do know. It's a powerful comfort.

I have a joke book, which is made up of titles of the world's shortest books. It includes such gems as 'What to do when your benefit cheque doesn't arrive by the Sultan of Brunei' 'The collected speeches of Marcel Marceau' and 'Darth Vader's guide to making and keeping friends'. But in the humour, there is a serious message and that message is that we can get alongside others and offer them real comfort but only if we have suffered ourselves.

Our situations do work together for good for us. God sees into eternity while we do not even know what tomorrow will bring. I find that God has a tendency of fitting together past events, situations, people and more to bring about something that could not occur without all that has gone before.

One Wednesday night, I woke up with the most horrendous pain in my calf. Like cramp but so much worse. It did not go away but I went to work on Thursday as usual. On Friday, the pain was still there. I felt God telling me I had DVT (deep vein thrombosis) and I should go to the doctor. I Googled DVT and sure enough, I had the symptoms. So I went to work and rang the doctors from my office. (I am very loathe to take time off work). They insisted I attend the surgery immediately. The doctor agreed I had enough symptoms to suggest I had DVT, a swollen leg, pain and I'd just done a long haul flight. The doctor warned me that if the clot moved, it could kill me. This was likely to have a huge impact on my life, how would I get travel insurance again? What was the likelihood I would ever do a long haul flight again? Would the clot move and suddenly kill me? Sitting in her surgery I felt oddly peaceful. I had an overwhelming conviction that God was in charge.

I was ordered to rest, take light exercise and advised that the district nurse would be round shortly to give me injections in my stomach. I was given an appointment for a scan at the local hospital, which would determine where the clot was and how big it was. I collected my prescription of injections from the chemist and waited for the nurse to arrive. The second day the nurse came to inject me she said I should learn to do it myself. Cue a scene worthy of the comedian Tony Hancock.

Me: "How far in does the needle go?"
Nurse "All the way".
Me: "Nooo. I have vital organs in there. What if I hit one?"
Nurse "You won't". Push the plunger and inject it all".
Me: "All except the bubble".
Nurse "All including the bubble".
Me: "Noooo".

I injected the bubble.
When I went to the hospital for a scan, there was no sign of a clot. No one could offer me an explanation as to what had caused the pain and swelling if not DVT. It didn't seem likely that I'd pulled a muscle in the middle of the night. Having told my employer that I would be off work for 3 to 6 months, I went straight back to work. The peace I had felt that day in doctor's surgery, had been right. I had nothing to worry about.
When we despair and say we can only see bad, that everything looks hopeless, aren't we claiming we know the future? Aren't we making ourselves out to be like God? God who is the only one who knows the future. When our lives seem to be falling apart, it may be that they are falling together.
If we believe that everything works together for good for those that love God, we need to accept that God is using our current situation. And that we're in the right place. God could have healed my friend that very first night. But it wouldn't have had the same impact on us. Jesus could

have rushed off to Bethany and healed Lazarus. But instead he turned up too late to heal but in time to raise him from the dead. Demanding that God gives us a small miracle now may mean that we're deprived of a big miracle later. If we do believe that God works everything for good for us, then we need to thank God for bad situations as well as good.

Chapter 11 Conclusion

Revelation 5 v 8 NIV

Twenty-four Elders fell down and worshiped the Lamb. Each had a harp and each had a bowl, a gold bowl filled with incense, the prayers of God's holy people.

Finding time to pray is often an issue for many people. People tell me they are too busy, that there isn't a quiet space or any undisturbed time. People often tell me that the only time they can find to pray is when they are driving to work. Seriously, if you had a friend who only found time to talk to you as long as they were doing something else as well, would you really consider you had a relationship with them? Imagine you ring them up for a chat and they say, ok, we can talk as long as you come in the car with me and we chat while I'm driving.
Or they say to come round when they're doing the washing up or the ironing so they have something to do while you both chat. But they never, ever stop what they are doing to just spend time with you. Would you feel that they value your relationship? That you are important to them? Would you honestly feel like doing

anything for them? I doubt it. I remember one Saturday, a friend of mine really needed to talk. I do try to drop everything to make space for people but on this Saturday I had promised to collect one of my teenagers from a nearby city.
The only option I could see was to take my friend along and chat as I drove, so we did. It still doesn't feel like an ideal solution, but it worked as a one off. If that was all I ever offered her, would we still be friends? Would she feel I was actually interested in her and what she had to say? Probably not. So why do so many us do this to God? We fit our prayer times in while we're doing something else.
I remember a sermon I once heard preached in which the preacher told us we could praise God in our everyday lives just by doing everyday tasks. He insisted we don't need to make anytime time for God, as long as we think about God while we go about our lives. He ended with this poem:

Lord of all pots and pans and things
Since I've no time to be
A saint by doing lovely things
Or watching late with Thee
Or dreaming in the sweet dawn light
Or storming Heaven's gates,
Make me a saint by getting meals
And washing up the plates.

Although I must have Martha's hands,
I have a Mary mind,
And when I black the boots and shoes,

Thy sandals, Lord, I find.
I think of how they trod the earth,
What time I scrub the floor:
Accept this meditation, Lord.
I haven't time for more.

Warm all the kitchen with Thy love
And light it with Thy peace;
Forgive me all my worrying,
And make all grumbling cease.
Thou who didst love to give men food,
In room or by the sea,
Accept this service that I do—
I do it unto Thee
Anon.

I cringe when I read these words 'I haven't time for more'. If we haven't got time for God can we seriously expect God to find time for us? After all, God has a whole universe to run. Yet, unbelievably, this poem not only tells God we don't have time for him it then goes on to tell him that we expect him to do stuff for us as this poem clearly does – words fail me.
It is of course, based on the story of Mary and Martha in Luke 10 v 38-42 NIV

As they continued their travel, Jesus entered a village. A woman by the name of Martha welcomed him and made him feel quite at home. She had a sister, Mary, who sat before the Master, hanging on every word he said. But Martha was pulled away by all she had to do in the kitchen. Later, she stepped in, interrupting

them. "Master, don't you care that my sister has abandoned the kitchen to me? Tell her to lend me a hand."
The Master said, "Martha, dear Martha, you're fussing far too much and getting yourself worked up over nothing. One thing only is essential, and Mary has chosen it—it's the main course, and won't be taken from her."

Martha was busying herself with preparing food while Mary was sitting and listening to Jesus. Martha remonstrated with Jesus, but he insisted that Mary had chosen right. After all, this was the same Jesus who fed 5,000 with one small boy's lunch. Did Martha really need to be spending time preparing food? I don't think so. I wonder how many of us are doing what we think needs doing, when we could just leave it God to sort out? Instead of worrying and trying to make things happen, we could just relax and remember that God knows what is needed. Did Martha do herself out of a miracle by insisting on staying in the kitchen? We'll never know. But please don't make the same mistake. Rather than trying to resolve a situation, rather than do what you think needs doing, rather than busy yourself. Why not try sitting and listening to God? Instead of worrying about everything that needs doing, why not just let go and let God?
I wonder how prevalent is this attitude that work is worship? I did an Internet search to try and find the poem and despite only remembering the line 'I haven't time for more' it was easy enough to find and alongside it a lots of comments and

platitudes about how busy our lives are and how God understands we don't have time available to only spend with him. Would we be as understanding if someone we loved told us that spending time with us simply wasn't a priority for them? Why do we think God won't mind? I find it sad when people say they don't have time to pray, that they don't have time spare. As if we only fit God into spare time. Or is that they consider time spent praying is wasted time? Time spent doing nothing. Nothing except communicating with God. How can that ever be wasted time?

The Bible quote at the start of this chapter is one of my favourites. Isn't it amazing that there are gold bowls in heaven filled with our prayers? When I pray I think of my prayers rising to heaven and blending with all the other prayers of God's people. Revelation describes prayers as being like incense. Incense of course, rises up and smells sweet. It is has been used as part of worship for thousands of years. Our prayers are like incense to God and smell sweet to him.

Clearly, we can only have a relationship with God if we make time to spend with him. This begs the question- is a really close relationship with God only available to those who have lots of spare time? A friend of mine recently asked her employer if she could work a four-day week, which would give her a day to spend in prayer. She can afford to do that. She earns more than 4 times the average income. What of those who do not have the luxury of leisure time? Parents with small children? Parents who get the kids off to school before going to work all day, coming home to cooking & house work? Carers who are never off duty from their caring responsibilities? Is spirituality not achievable for them? Far from it. When we prioritise time spent with God, he recognises and values that time. When I was at home with a baby and a toddler and running a small business, it was hard to find time to pray.

In the evenings my two older children came home from school and my husband came home from work. He wasn't a Christian so didn't understand that spending time praying was important to me. I don't think it would have gone down well if I'd left him with all four children while I spent time praying. Instead, I found small amounts of time throughout the day. It was tempting to use that time to do things, which are difficult with toddlers, like washing the kitchen floor or making business phone calls. But I put prayer on my list of priorities, along with washing the kitchen floor and chose to spend some of that time with God. On days when I didn't get the choice, I would snatch five minutes here and there and found they soon mounted up. As my children got older, God pointed out to me that the house was quiet between 6.30am and 7am.

If my husband was on the day shift, he left before 6.30am and if he was working nights, he didn't get home until after 7am and the kids never got up before 7am. The only problem was that while the kids didn't get up before 7am, nor did I. Getting up at 6.30am was hard at first. I would drag myself out of bed only to fall asleep on the sofa. But I persevered. I wanted to spend time with God. I soon found myself keen to get up and spend time with God.

Mark 12 v 41 The Message
Sitting across from the offering box, he was observing how the crowd tossed money in for the collection. Many of the rich were making large contributions. One poor widow came up and put in two small coins—a measly two cents. Jesus called his disciples over and said, "The truth is that this poor widow gave more to the collection than all the others put together. All the others gave what they'll never miss; she gave extravagantly what she couldn't afford—she gave her all."

She put in more because she gave all she has. It isn't the actual amount of time that we spend it's how much of our free time we are prepared to use. This isn't a competition that those with the luxury of leisure time will win. We do need to be aware that our purpose on earth isn't to spend every moment with our sole focus on God. We shouldn't be neglecting other people to spend more time with God. We need to find a balance. Being human, we all too often allow ourselves to go to one extreme or the other. Read what Jesus said in Matthew 22 v 37-40

"'Love the Lord your God with all your passion and prayer and intelligence.' This is the most important, the first on any list. But there is a second to set alongside it: 'Love others as well as you love yourself.' These two commands are pegs; everything in God's Law and the Prophets hangs from them."

Love God, but love other people too. We aren't meant to lock ourselves away and spend every moment with God; we need to love people too.

If praying everyday or if thanking God instead of asking are new for you, take it slowly. There's no requirement to start with 30 mins a day. Here's some advice I found on the internet on starting to exercise but it's just as relevant for starting to pray:

'Here is a little secret. When I first started exercising, I did it with five minutes per day, three times a week. Can you imagine that? Five minutes of timed exercise, three times a week? That's nothing, you might be thinking. And you are right, because the task is so easy and anyone can succeed with it, you can really start to make a habit out of it.'.

I know I started praying with 5 minutes a day. Praying for 5 minutes 3 times a day is the same as praying once for 15 minutes. Yet praying for 15 minutes a day may well sound too much of a challenge.

Don't put off spending time with God because you don't have the luxury of leisure. Give something up. For me, it's sleep. What will you give up? If you give willingly to God, then he will give in return. I was intrigued to hear a radio news report, which claimed that new research shows that walking 30 mins a day extends a person's life by 30 mins. So it seems the time Ispend prayer walking will be given back to me. How amazing is that? It is not always easy to find time, but it is always possible to make time. If we really want to spend time with God, we will make time. How many of us give God leftover time? If we are serious about building a relationship with him we need to give God what's right, not what's left.

As the months passed and I continued to praise walk around my friend's school. My friend began to report that the school was becoming a different place. She was no longer desperate to leave and staff turnover has lessened. She told me she was increasingly finding opportunities to share her faith. The deputy head asked her to get him a Bible and a teaching assistant reported hearing angels singing 'Hallelujah'. The school is now due to be knocked down and rebuilt which is great news as they have squeezed a preschool in, but it is has made the school too cramped. I was particularly thrilled to hear that the school has put prayer at the centre of their school day. It began with the staff holding weekly prayer meetings, and then they put a prayer request box in each classroom for the children to drop in prayer requests. The requests are taken to the parish church to be included in the church prayers. But recently, the school has started a prayer meeting for the children, where they pray over the requests in the box too. The school also ran an Alpha course for the oldest class.

Funny really, because I haven't asked for any of

these things, I haven't asked God for anything. I have simply walked round the school praising God and thanking him for the school.

It's not just the school that has benefited. One morning I spotted a photo ID in the street. Presuming it belonged to a 6th former at the local school, as the strap was the same colour as theirs, I picked it up. It was a staff member's ID from a hospital. I put in my pocket intending to phone the number on the back of the ID when I noticed a police car outside a house just a few houses down. I stopped and yes, they'd just been burglared and yes, the ID was theirs. The owner was so pleased to get it back she hugged me.

I mentioned at the beginning that my dog accompanies on my praise walking. He's an Akita/Bull Mastiff cross that we got from a rescue. 9 stone of boundless enthusiasm, it wasn't unusual for people to be nervous of him. Now the phrase most people use to describe him is peaceful. And he is. He hasn't lost his boundless enthusiasm, he still loves everyone & everything, but he is peaceful. He's also very happy as he now gets a morning walk double the length of the walk he used to get.

How we worship God is not important. Different people have different ways of worshipping God. All that matters is that we do worship him.

God has a plan for our lives but he also gives us free will. We aren't forced down a certain path. We make our own choices. There are times when those choices are not the best and times when they take us down a different path. When we make these choices, God does not abandon us, but like a sat nav, he recalculates our route. When my friend was seriously ill, her children were only six years old and nine years old. I believe that had we failed to pray for her, God would have recalculated the lives of those two children to make up for the loss of their Mum. God's plan for me was to be brought up by two loving parents. They made their own choices, which didn't involve doing the best for me. God stepped in and provided replacements.

What I hope you have taken from this book is that we should stop concentrating on our problems and ourselves when we pray. Our focus must be on God. When we do pray asking prayers, they should be on behalf of others and not for ourselves.

A BBC Radio 4 programme which tried to investigate the power of prayer came across someone who did an experiment in retrospective prayer. They took the medical notes of several people who had been admitted to hospital, divided the notes into two piles and then prayed for one pile. After praying, they then looked at the outcomes for each patient. The patients in the 'prayed for' pile had significantly better outcomes than the not prayed for pile. The programme maker derided this as absolute nonsense. But for those of us, who have a God who lives outside of time and who listens to our prayers, is it so ludicrous?

Luke chapter 19 verses 35-40. The Message.

They brought the colt to Jesus. Then, throwing their coats on its back, they helped Jesus get on. As he rode, the people gave him a grand welcome, throwing their coats on the street.
Right at the crest, where Mount Olives begins its descent, the whole crowd of disciples burst into enthusiastic praise over all the mighty works they had witnessed:
Blessed is he who comes, the king in God's name! All's well in heaven! Glory in the high places!
Some Pharisees from the crowd told him, "Teacher, get your disciples under control!"
But he said, "If they kept quiet, the stones would do it for them, shouting praise."

If we don't praise God then the stones will cry out. Don't let your place be taken by a stone. Instead, why not fill those gold bowls in heaven with your praises?

How incredible is the thought that God keeps our prayers in golden bowls by his throne and they smell like incense? Surely we should try and ensure that our prayers will smell sweet to God? Isn't the surest way to do that, to praise more than we ask?

Printed in Great Britain
by Amazon